Criminal Justice
Recent Scholarship

Edited by
Marilyn McShane and Frank P. Williams III

A Series from LFB Scholarly

Crime and Community Policing

M. Alper Sozer

LFB Scholarly Publishing LLC
El Paso 2009

Library of Congress Cataloging-in-Publication Data

Sozer, M. Alper, 1977-
  Crime and community policing / M. Alper Sozer.
      p. cm. -- (Criminal justice : recent scholarship)
  Includes bibliographical references and index.
  ISBN 978-1-59332-379-0 (hardcover : alk. paper)
  1. Community policing--United States--Research. 2. Crime
prevention--United States--Research. I. Title.
  HV7936.C83S69 2009
  363.2'3--dc22

                                    2009022781

ISBN 978-1-59332-379-0

Printed on acid-free 250-year-life paper.

Manufactured in the United States of America.

Dedication

To my wife Özlem and our three sons.

Contents

Acknowledgements

Knowledge is to understand
To understand who you are
If you know not who you are
What's the use of learning

Yunus Emro (1240-1320)

In the process of writing this book, numerous people whose names cannot be listed within a single page have helped me in many ways.. However, I should mention here two most important supporters. First, I would like to express my greatest appreciation to the Turkish taxpayers and the Turkish government for their financial support during my stay in the U.S. Second, I would like to extend my grateful appreciation to Dr. Merlo, who has encouraged, supported, and assisted me throughout my work.

CHAPTER 1

The Question of Decades: Is it Working?

The history of policing in the U.S. has been classified into three eras by Kelling & Moore (1988): the political era, the reform era, and the community policing era. In the political era, the police were tightly linked to local politicians. "Police helped ward political leaders maintain their political efforts by encouraging citizens to vote for certain candidates, discouraging them for voting others, and at times, by assisting in rigging elections" (Kelling & Moore, 1988, p. 3). During the reform era, the philosophy of good policing focused on visibility of patrols, quick response time, and the success of follow-up investigations (Goldstein, 1990). Crime fighting was viewed as the sole responsibility of police, and the means of policing overshadowed the ends of policing. In this era, "the deterrent capacity of police has been largely overestimated and traditional police response exaggerated" (Greene & Taylor, 1988 p. 196). However, public dissatisfaction with the police services coupled with increase in crime generated criticism that the reform era of policing had failed to produce the expected results.

As a response to this outcry, governments, scholars, and agencies sought innovative strategies that could successfully reduce crime and improve police and community relations. There are a number of innovative policing strategies aimed at improving police performance: "community policing", "broken windows policing", "problem-oriented policing", "pulling levers policing", "third-party policing", "hot spots policing", "Compstat", and "evidence-based policing" (Braga & Weisburd, 2006). Among these, community policing, which influenced policing strategies not only in the U.S., but also in many other countries throughout the world (Lab & Das, 2003), has been the most popular trend during the past few decades (MacDonald, 2002; Palmiotto, 2000; Skogan, 2006).

Although scholars and professionals have not reached consensus on a single definition for community policing, many programs under the rubric of community policing have surfaced since the 1970s. Initially, community policing was adapted by a few large agencies in major American cities in the form of a pilot study. In general, studies during that time mostly yielded positive results. Those positive results included a reduced fear of crime, improved public-police relationships, and the prevention of crime (Lindsey & McGilis, 1986; Police Foundation, 1981; Schneider, 1978; Skogan & Wycoff, 1986; Tien & Cahn, 1986). It did not take long for the positive results revealed in data from sample sites to attract the attention of politicians. Governor Bill Clinton, during his presidential campaign in Detroit, Michigan, recognized community policing as a solution to the increase in reported crime. In 1992, he declared that "it is time for America to make a serious commitment to community policing, to having people back on the beat, working the same neighborhood, making relationships with people in ways that prevent crime" (Reed, 1999, p. 3).

When elected, President Clinton proposed legislation which included a provision to put 100,000 new officers on the streets to strengthen the community policing initiative. The Violent Crime Control and Law Enforcement Act of 1994 provided law enforcement agencies nearly 9 billion dollars for hiring officers and supporting innovative practices and new technology. Community policing rapidly became a widespread phenomenon (Gest, 2001). With federal support, community policing began to be adopted in small and rural departments as well. The percentage of departments employing community policing personnel increased from 34% in 1997 to 64% in 1999 (Hickman & Reaves, 2003). "On May 12, 1999, the White House announced that the goal of funding 100,000 officers had been met" (Roth & Ryan, 2000, p. 15).

According to Hickman and Reaves (2006), the number of community policing officers peaked in the year 2000; and then, slowly decreased through 2003. Since the Office of Community Oriented Policing Services' (COPS) funds for hiring new community policing officers were good for only three years, these fluctuations in numbers are not surprising. It was well established that at the end of the third year, agencies had to sustain employees by their own resources. The funding success was evident in the dramatic increase in the number of community policing officers in 2003 compared to the 1997 level (Hickman & Reaves, 2006). By the end of the fiscal year 2004, COPS funded more than 118,768 community policing officers and deputies, and the total investment of COPS reached $11.3 billion (COPS, 2007).

Does allocating such a large amount of money for supporting law enforcement agencies to implement community policing affect the incidence of crime on a national level? According to the *Uniform Crime Report* (UCR), crime has been consistently declining since 1993 (Federal Bureau of Investigation [FBI], 2006). Scholars have suggested that community policing might have a general role in the last decade's crime drop (Marvel & Moody, 1996; Zhao, Schreider, & Thurman, 2002; Zhao & Thurman, 2004). Contrastingly, some scholars argued that it is difficult to claim that this reduction was attributable to community policing since many other positive social factors that might influence crime such as an improved economy and high employment were evident during the 1990s (Bayley, 1998a; Eck & Maguire, 2000). Studies controlling other factors such as incarceration rates and sentencing policies also yielded contradictory results (Government Accountability Office [GAO], 2003, 2005; Muhlhausen, 2001).

Despite the fact that these findings are inconclusive, Braga and Weisburd (2006) contend that the future of policing will be community oriented regardless of alterations in technology and policing strategy. Therefore, more research and knowledge about the effects of community policing on crime are vital in order to guide future policing policies.

The Previous Studies

Early studies about the effectiveness of community policing were limited to large cities (Bowers & Hirsch, 1987; Fowler, McCalla, & Mangione, 1979; Kessler & Duncan, 1996; Lindsey & McGilis, 1986; Pate, McPherson, Silloway, 1987; Schneider, 1978; Skogan & Wycoff, 1986; Tien & Cahn, 1986; Uchida, Forst, Annan, 1992; Wycoff & Skogan, 1993). The framework and implementation of community policing strategies varied from one department to another, but the use of foot patrol as a community policing activity was the most prominent characteristic. These studies examined the effects of community policing through pre-test/ post-test or a single post-test with or without comparison groups (Lurigio & Rosenbaum, 1986; Yin, 1986). According to Kessler & Duncan (1996), the majority of these studies suffered because of weak research designs. They underused statistical significance tests and measured concepts poorly. These studies lacked a valid and reliable measure of program implementation and outcomes, and they consistently failed to address competing explanations for observed effects (Eck & Maguire, 2000; Levitt, 2004; Lurigio & Rosenbaum, 1986).

After a significant federal investment in community policing, national studies began to appear in the literature. When Zhao, Schreider, and Thurman (2002) examined the effects of COPS funds on crime, it was the first study of its kind. However, the GAO (2003) criticized their study for its methodology and the validity of its findings. Zhao & Thurman (2004) revised their study in view of the criticisms, and they found nearly the same results. Later, the GAO (2005) conducted its own study to address methodological flaws in previous studies. Like Zhao & Thurman (2004), the GAO concluded that COPS' funds reduced crime nationwide.

Roth, Roehl, and Johnson (2004) asserted that "the ultimate test of community policing can be achieved by investigating whether local crime levels fall after an agency adopts community policing practices" (p. 26). By 2003, the majority of departments, particularly large departments, had already adopted some type of community policing practices. Therefore, in contemporary studies, the main focus should be to what extent community policing can influence the level of crime in associated jurisdictions. In short, whether an agency adopted community policing should no longer be considered a priority in measuring the effect of community policing on crime. Nonetheless, the operationalization of community policing was inadequate in these studies even though they included small departments and large departments in their analyses. Palmiotto and Donahue (1995) contend that there must be evidence presenting the level of implementation to thoroughly assess the impact of community policing on any outcome measure.

There were two studies which used some indications of community policing. For example, MacDonald (2002) used a dichotomous variable and a summated index to operationalize community policing activities in agencies. He examined their effects only on two types of violent crime (murder and robbery) within the urban context. Beckman (2006), on the other hand, took a different approach and used a variety of activities to operationalize community policing. She created eight subgroups of community policing activities and looked at the differences between each subgroup in terms of their associated change in crime rates. However, like MacDonald (2002), she excluded small departments in her analysis, and there was no discussion regarding the reliability of each subgroup in measuring community policing. Nonetheless, these two studies presented some evidence of implementation, but they overlooked small departments. As Wells & Weisheit (2004) noted:

> If there are fundamental rural/urban differences in the process by which crime is generated, then focusing almost exclusively on urban areas amounts to little more than convenience sampling in which important sources of variation are omitted. The fact that rural areas can be difficult to study is not a justification for excluding them from research. (p. 20)

What difference are we making?

Previous studies have failed to examine the impact of community policing by simultaneously taking the level of implementation and various agency sizes into consideration. With this limitation as a foundation, this book examines the relationship between the level of implementation of community policing and crime rates by considering variations across agency size with the most recent data available.

First, this study conducts analyses on a combined data set that consists of two national data sets (UCR & Census) along with data collected at the national level through a sample survey of Law Enforcement Management and Administrative Statistics (LEMAS). Second, unlike most of the previous research, this study employs scales in order to identify the level of implementation of community policing in the agencies instead of just using a dichotomous variable. Third, variables that are well-known correlates of crime such as poverty, urban population, and female single headed households are used to control socioeconomic characteristics of the jurisdictions. Fourth, this study analyzes agencies serving populations that are fewer than 50,000 and over 50,000 separately in order to see if there are differences between these two different populations. Multiple-regression are employed as the primary statistical technique to determine if there is an association between community policing and crime rates.

Chapter II begins with the introduction of policing history. First, the theoretical background and definition of community policing are discussed. Second, community policing in practice is reviewed through the four major objectives of community policing identified by COPS (Roth & Ryan, 2000).

In Chapter III, previous studies are reviewed together with their methodological strengths and, limitations by dividing them into two different groups: research prior to the institutionalization phase and research from the institutionalization phase to the present within the context of Oliver's (2000) definition of "the evolution of community policing". In the chapter's conclusion, the justification for including small departments in the analysis is discussed.

Chapter IV provides an explanation of the methodology of this book. It starts with an overview of research design, research questions, and hypotheses. The data sets and linking strategy are also discussed. The rationale for inclusion of the variables is addressed along with the procedures that will be followed to generate the scales that measure the implementation of community policing.

In Chapter V, the measures of level of implementation of community policing are generated. Then, these composite measures are further analyzed for their reliability and validity. Second, OLS regression analysis is conducted to determine whether there is an association between the level of implementation of community policing and crime rates. Finally, whether this association differs based on the size of the agencies is investigated. In Chapter VI, the findings of the analyses are discussed and possible policy implications are presented. Finally, the limitations of this research are delineated and directions for future research are suggested.

CHAPTER 2

Community Policing

THE ROOT OF MODERN POLICING

The history of policing can be traced back to ancient Egypt and Mesopotamia (Adamson, 1991). However, in this book, as in a number of others (Carter & Radelet, 1999; Miller & Hess, 2002; Ortmeier, 2002; Peak & Glensor, 2004; Walker & Katz, 2005), the year 1829, when the London Metropolitan Police was founded by Sir Robert Peel, is used as the origin of modern policing.

Between 1600 and 1800, England experienced a significant population increase along with diversity and social change. The English population grew from roughly 4 million to 8.5 million (Bryant, 2006). It was the period of rapid structural change in the economy that simultaneously resulted in many rich and poor people in society (Crafts, 1977). English elites were particularly concerned about being victimized by crime because poor and unemployed people dominated London streets (Johnson, 1981).

The English Parliament appointed Sir Robert Peel as a chief of London Metropolitan Police after a parliamentary commission had failed to solve crime problems (Carter & Radelet, 1999). Peel proposed that London's crime problem required a full-time paid and professional police force. Parliament, despite strong opposition, enacted the Metropolitan Police Act of 1829. Subsequently, the first full-time, paid, and sworn officers were dispatched to London's streets to maintain the order and prevent crime (Champion & Rush, 1997).

Peel perceived that the one of the major reasons of social disorder was the poor quality of policing (Peak & Glensor, 2004, p. 2). In order to improve the quality of policing, he established his renowned nine police principles, which are still largely accepted as a foundation of modern policing and essentials of community policing (Carter & Radelet, 1999; Champion & Rush, 1997; Stevens, 2003; Peak & Radelet, 1999; Champion & Rush, 1997; Stevens, 2003; Peak & Glensor, 2004). Peel's emphasis on the relationship between community and police is noteworthy as it is closely related to today's community policing philosophy. "Peel recognized that the police were only successful at their jobs when they elicited public approval and assistance in their actions without resorting to force or severity of law. No police department can control crime and disorder without the consent and voluntary compliance by the public" (Keith, 2002, p. 111).

The History of American Policing

In America, early police duties were performed by night watchmen, constables, and sheriffs (Carter & Radelet, 1999). During the Revolutionary War, peacekeeping was maintained by the militia and troops (Palmiotto, 2000). When industrialization and social issues required professional policing, Americans replicated the London experience. American cities, like London witnessed disorder, riots, and violence. Moreover, racial conflicts, conflicts among immigrants, financial crises, and political clashes created an environment in which crimes were everyday occurrences in the lives of people living in cities such as New York, Baltimore, and Philadelphia (Miller& Huss, 2002).

In the midst of all this, the first full-time paid preventive police force was established in New York City in 1845. The night and day watchmen shifts were consolidated. Police officers in the New York City Police Department neither wore uniforms nor carried guns until the mid 1850s (Palmiotto, 2000). They served as servants of the public. Their major duties were supplying coal to the poor, sweeping streets, keeping girls away from prostitution, and helping overnight lodging services (Carter & Radelet, 1999). Other major cities followed the model; and by 1857, Boston, Philadelphia, Baltimore, Cincinnati, New Orleans, and Chicago had consolidated police departments (Miller & Hess, 2002).

Despite the fact that the new style of policing was modeled after London, there were three distinctive differences between American and English policing. First, American policing although technically centralized, functioned as a decentralized force in neighborhoods. "Cities were divided into precincts, and precinct-level managers often, in concert with ward leaders, ran precincts as small-scale departments"

(Kelling & Moore, 1988, p. 5). In London, the police force was centralized and functioned under the authority of a police chief (Peak & Glensor, 2004; Stevens, 2003). Second, in America, police management was placed under the control of city governments and politicians, and they dominanted police chiefs in terms of managing and appointing police officers. By contrast, in England, central authority was appointed by Crown, and the police chief had authority to manage and discipline officers (Kelling & Moore, 1988). Third, American policing focused on maintaining security and enforcing law, while the main focus of English policing was maintaining peace and crime prevention (Stevens, 2003).

The Political Era
Kelling & Moore (1988) categorize the period from 1840 to the early 1900s as the "political era" of policing in the United States. Unlike England, policing was closely tied to politics in America during this period. The police and the politicians collaborated to control the wards. The main focus of police forces was to protect the interests of politicians rather than to conduct professional police operations. The quality of police operations at the time was far from professional (Miller & Huss, 2002). The communication between foot patrol and headquarters was almost non-existent, and police chiefs did not have control over their precincts. Police officers usually resided in neighborhoods in their beats; and each precinct was dominated by a particular ethnic group which resulted in discrimination against other ethnic and racial groups. Nevertheless, "police were integrated in neighborhoods and enjoyed the support of at least the dominant and economically powerful groups" (Palmiotto, 2000, p. 25).

The Reform Era
In the beginning of the 20th century, American policing shifted from public service to crime fighting. Stevens (2003) claimed that Prohibition and the Great Depression of the 1930s were the impetus for this shift. However, the origin of this shift can be traced back to August Vollmer, the Chief of Police of Berkeley, California, who suggested that crime fighting is the most important duty of police. Vollmer's innovations in American policing are also viewed as the beginning of the "reform era" (Kelling and Moore, 1988), which is also known as the "professionalization movement" according to Walker & Katz (2005).

According to Stevens (2003), it was hypothesized that the police should be professionals in order to become more effective in fighting crime. Furthermore, additional education was perceived as a key element for effective policing, Vollmer successfully convinced the University of California-Berkeley to offer academic training for police cadets for the first time in the nation (Champion & Rush, 1997). Vollmer's innovations for the profession changed the cadets' perceptions toward their jobs and enabled them to view this profession as a career.

Rapid response time and calls for service were among the top priorities of the police in the reform era. Technologies such as two way radios and patrol cars improved the effectiveness of police in terms of fighting crime by enhancing communication and reducing response time (Champion & Rush, 1997). Orlando Winfield Wilson, one of Vollmer's protégés, continued Vollmer's innovations and contributed to police management by formulating assignments of patrol officers according to their workloads. "His emphasis on efficiency was the major influence in the basic shift of American policing from foot patrol to automobile patrol" (Walker & Katz, 2005, p. 41). However, as time progressed, those innovations were viewed as contributing factors to police – community alienation (Peak & Glensor, 2004; Stevens, 2003; Walker & Katz, 2005).

Another characteristic of the reform era is that it helped to insulate police departments from political influence. The political patronage of hiring and firing police officers was partly eliminated, and the crime fighting role of police dominated (Palmiotto, 2000). Civil service roles of the police like fire fighting and responding to medical emergency calls were transferred to fire departments and emergency call units (Ortmeier, 2002). "Police professionalism was defined almost exclusively in terms of managerial efficiency, and administrators sought to further strengthen their hand in controlling rank-and-file officers" (Peak & Glensor, 2004, p. 10).

Conversely, the professionalization movement created an isolated environment for police. Distant policing assumed the citizens to be passive recipients, whose roles in crime control were making calls and serving as witnesses (Peak & Glensor, 2004; Stevens, 2003). Consequently, the term the "thin blue line" emerged. It refers to the line that separates law-abiding citizens from predators, and police from the public they serve. It implies not only police heroism but also police loneliness (Kelling & Moore, 1988).

During the reform era, the relationship between community and police was really remote. Later, commissions questioned the criminal justice system and verified this alienation between police and the community. The National Commission on Law Observance and Enforcement (NCLOE), also known as the Wickersham Commission, conducted the first national study on the criminal justice system in 1931. The study revealed that police used excessively brutal methods while investigating crime in order to obtain confessions or statements (NCLOE, 1931). Moreover, the Wickersham Commission recommended establishing higher standards in recruiting police officers and training, which had already started to be implemented in agencies under the control of Vollmer and Wilson (Champion & Rush, 1997).

The next noteworthy change in American policing was J. Edgar Hoover's appointment as Director of the FBI in 1924. He took a highly corrupt agency and promoted the professional features of policing in the agency. He increased the Bureau's jurisdictions and gained enormous power over local police departments (Gest, 2001). "The introduction of the UCR, ten most wanted list, and the creation of crime labs all served to emphasize crime fighting at the expense of other aspects of policing" (Walker & Katz, 2005, p. 42).

In spite of the professional movement, crime continued to increase, especially between the 1960s and 1970s (Ortmeier, 2002). In the 1960s, the nation was in flux. Inner cities, where African Americans had dominated, witnessed riots against racial inequalities; and minorities specifically complained about police practices unfairly targeting African Americans. African Americans were followed by other citizens who marched on the streets to demonstrate their dissatisfaction with the government regarding the Vietnam War and civil rights issues. "During this time, Americans watched police on television respond to anti-war and civil rights demonstrations and were shocked at the treatment of students and minorities by the police" (Peak & Glensor, 2004, p. 12).

The changes in public administration were reflected in Supreme Court decisions about police practices. Three paramount cases were crucial in illustrating these changes. In *Mapp v. Ohio* (1961) the U.S. Supreme Court ruled that evidence gathered through an illegal search and seizure could not be used against the defendant. In *Katz v. United States* (1967) the U.S. Supreme Court ruled that physical trespass was not an essential element in judging the Fourth Amendment violation. Finally, in *Miranda v. Arizona* (1966) the U.S. Supreme Court ruled that police officers were required to provide the suspect notice of his/her rights before questioning. All of these three cases placed restrictions and new regulations on police practices.

These new trends in policing had not met the expectations of the public or the police, and the police were criticized. Kelling & Moore (1988) summarized these criticisms:

> First, rapid response time and mobilized patrolling failed to control or prevent crime. Second, fear of crime increased as well as crime itself. Third, objective treatment was not experienced by all segments of society. Fourth, civil rights and anti-war movements challenged the police and its legitimacy. Fifth, it was unfolded that crime fighting was the least practiced function of the police. Sixth, reform ideology was limited to management while line officers failed to embrace it. Seventh, fiscal difficulties of cities caused budget minimization in police departments. Finally, the rise of private security competed with police departments. (pp. 8-9)

As a result, the government took action and established national commissions to find solutions to the problems. In 1965, the second national study was conducted by the President's Commission on Law Enforcement and Administration of Justice (PCLEAJ) also known as the President's Commission. The President's Commission revealed that police should have higher recruitment standards, more training, and better management (PCLEAJ, 1967). After the riots of 1967, another commission, The National Advisory Commission on Civil Disorder (NACCD), also known as the Kerner Commission, was created to study racial issues. The Kerner Commission (1968) concluded that conflict between police and minorities was the main cause of the riots in big cities. Therefore, it was recommended that police departments eliminate aggressive crime fighting techniques such as frisks and frequent stops that created much of the tension between police and the minorities. The Commission also advocated hiring more African Americans and for the development of a professional process for citizen complaints (NACCD, 1968).

Based on the recommendations of these Commissions, Congress enacted the Omnibus Crime Control Act of 1968. One of its provisions was the creation of the Law Enforcement Assistant Administration (LEAA). Through LEAA, millions of dollars were spent on research as well as training programs and new equipment for law enforcement agencies (Champion & Rush, 1997). In the meantime, civil foundations such as the American Bar Association, the Ford Foundation, and the Police Executive Research Forum funded major studies on policing. The most notable of these was the Kansas City Preventive Patrol Experiment. In 1973, the third commission, The National Advisory Commission on Criminal Justice Standards and Goal (NACCJSG) promulgated a series of recommendations including the function of police in the community. Stevens (2003) argues that one common point among the three reports was the emphasis on better community and police relations, which might result in controlling violence and civil disorder (p. 10).

The Community Policing Era

The focus on community-police relationships spurred community involvement in policing efforts. It was believed that information that flowed from the community to the police could enhance police effectiveness, and information could be best gathered by patrol officers. In the 1970s, foot patrol regained popularity (Peak & Glensor, 2004; Stevens, 2003). Several studies showed that foot patrol increased citizen satisfaction with police, reduced fear of crime, and improved the community's relationship with the police (Police Foundation, 1981; Trojanowicz, 1983). In addition, police started to respond to the needs and the wishes of the community they served (Miller & Huss, 2002). Traditional policing, which primarily involved responding to calls for service, was no longer considered an indicator of good policing.

Even though the Kerner Commission report (1968), Radelet's workshops and studies on police community relations from 1965 to 1973 at the National Center on Police and Community Relations in Michigan State University, and the works of Germann (1969) and Angell (1971) served as the foundation of community policing, the seminal work of Goldstein (1977) is widely accepted as the beginning of a new era in policing. According to Goldstein (1977), police should work proactively rather than just respond to calls for services in order to find out the underlying causes that generate calls for service. In this new mode of policing, community participation was an essential part of identifying and solving problems.

During the same time, another seminal work by Wilson & Kelling (1982) emphasized that traditional policing failed to control crime. They found that police patrol had little deterrent effect on criminals, quick response time did not increase the chance of arrest, and detectives' investigation did not really help to solve the crime. Wilson & Kelling (1982) argued that effective policing heavily relied on citizens. Targeting incivilities and quality of life problems in the neighborhood could prevent more serious crime and reduce the fear of crime among residents. Miller and Huss (2002) observed that:

> At the heart of most new approaches to policing is a return to the ancient idea of community responsibility for the welfare of society... as Sir Robert Peel stated: 'The police are the public and the public are the police'. Policing has strayed so far from this principle in the past century that the concepts central to community policing seem fresh and sensible today. (p. 15)

Community policing promised to reconnect the police and the community. It is a philosophy based on enhancing community participation, enhancing rank and file officers' decision making authority, and targeting specific problems that prompt frequent calls for service. Accountability of police practices is also embedded in the community policing philosophy. Public confidence in the police is one of the key elements in gaining public support and cooperation in fighting crime, which, in turn, promotes police legitimacy (Ortmeier, 2002).

Community policing strategies were initiated in many police departments in the 1980s. However, its institutionalization process started with the enactment of The Violent Crime Control and Law Enforcement Act of 1994 (Oliver, 2000). Accordingly, the COPS office was established and allocated nearly 9 billion dollars to hire 100,000 new officers nationwide (Gest, 2001). Even though which types of activities each agency implemented for community policing were not clear, many departments received federal funds by claiming that they had some type of community policing program (Walker & Katz, 2005).

Theoretical Framework

The imprecision of the definition, concept, and construct of community policing has generated extensive debate among scholars in regard to how community policing is to be researched (Colvin & Goh, 2006; Cheurprakobkit, 2002). Community policing is theoretically immature and is not based on a dominant theory (Leighton, 1991; Maguire & Mastrofski, 2000). Despite these limitations, it has been argued that a number of theories and philosophies together form a background for it.

Due to incidents such as the Watergate scandal, the Vietnam War, and the Civil Rights movement, the public started to question the trustworthiness of the government. In particular, the conflict between minority groups and the police created a legitimacy crisis (Walker & Katz, 2005). The gap between the police and the community was revealed in a number of reports and supported by scholarly studies (Carter & Radelet, 1999; Department of Justice [DOJ], 1973; NACCD, 1968; Ortmeier, 2002). In addition, it was realized that policing was a complex issue and required more than just responding to calls for service. The lack of community support coupled with the limitations of traditional policing methods made it impossible for police forces to handle these problems effectively.

Simultaneously, criminological research focused on social and economic factors (Burgess & Akers, 1966; Clinard, 1964; Cloward & Ohlin, 1960; Kornhauser, 1978; Quinney, 1973; Turk, 1966; Wilson, 1975). Based upon the published studies of the 1960s and 1970s, the primary causes of crime were perceived as being out of the scope of police interests; and the belief that "it was unrealistic to expect the police to deal with the crime problem by themselves" dominated this period (White, 2007, p. 102). All these factors together influenced changes in policing. In this atmosphere, the community became a dominant character in police work. The seminal work of Goldstein's (1990) problem-oriented policing along with Wilson and Kelling's (1982) "broken windows" theory are the cornerstones of the transition in policing from the reform era to the community policing era (Oliver, 2000).

Problem-oriented Policing Philosophy

Goldstein (1977) argued that traditional police tactics were no longer useful for effective policing and that a radical change was necessary. He contended that the professional model of policing must shift from incident based to problem based. Instead of responding to a single incident, the main focus of policing was to identify underlying causes of problems in the community and to work with the community to solve them (Goldstein, 1990). The police should identify the causes of problems before the crime occurs. Thus, the response to crime has to be proactive rather than reactive. Identifying and solving community problems rely heavily on citizen involvement. Police should engage with the community and communicate with residents effectively in order to identify the underlying causes of a problem. Then, the police will be able to help the community overcome its own problems (Miller & Hess, 2002).

Broken Windows Theory
Wilson and Kelling (1982) argue that there is an important relationship between disorder and crime. Therefore, they contend that police should focus on the disorder that affects the quality of life in the neighborhood. Their broken windows theory states that incivilities and disorder exacerbate the fear of crime which, in turn, weakens the social cohesion in the neighborhood. If there are physical and social signs that reveal that a particular area is unattended, other kinds of disorder might be attracted to that area. When panhandlers, prostitutes, loitering youths, and drug dealers start to occupy the neighborhood, law-abiding families move out, and other law-abiding citizens, who cannot leave the neighborhood, start withdrawing from active participation in neighborhood activities (Wilson & Kelling, 1982). Overall, this climate makes the neighborhood crime prone, and more serious crimes are likely to occur.

According to broken windows theory, social cohesion and community involvement are key factors to eliminate physical and social signs of incivilities from the neighborhood. By working closely with the community, police should remove signs of incivility from the neighborhood and proactively prevent crime (Wilson & Kelling, 1982).

Broken windows theory has two major drawbacks. First, Matthews (1992) argued that there is no relationship between crime and disorder. Second, the crime and disorder relationship is spurious as "collective efficacy" is superior and affects both disorder and crime (Sampson & Raudenbush, 1999). However, research examining structural relationships between disorder and crime and community policing found that the "moral decay of community may indeed lead to more crime, and that other things such as collective efficacy being equal, fixing broken windows may be the best thing the police and community can do to prevent crime" (Xu, Fiedler, & Flaming, 2005, p. 174).

Social Disorganization Theory
Alternatively, Adams, Rohe, and Arcury (2005) argued that Shaw and McKay's (1942) theory of social disorganization suggests a set of solutions which serve as fundamental principles and a theoretical background for almost all community based crime prevention programs. High residential mobility, heterogeneity of the population, poverty, and constant social change weaken neighborhood residents' social control and allow a value system nurtured by crime to emerge. Moreover, this value system is transferred to the next generation through interactions among neighborhood residents (Shaw & McKay, 1942). As a result, neighborhoods lose their collective efficacy to fight against disorder and crime (Cullen & Agnew, 2004; Sampson & Grove, 1989).

Shaw and McKay (1942) advocated that agencies work with the community residents in order to build a sense of community that takes care of its own problems and provides social control. In their project (The Chicago Area Project), Shaw and McKay created recreational programs and worked with criminal justice officials to find ways to help delinquent youth. A part of this project involved using community residents to counsel youth in the neighborhood. Although social disorganization theory is not directly linked to community policing, they do share common elements such as collaboration and the shared responsibility with the community to maintain order. These are crucial elements of both. Therefore, utilizing social disorganization as one theoretical framework for community policing has some merit. As the International Association of Chiefs of Police Crime Prevention Committee stated, "Community safety is everyone's responsibility and crime prevention is everyone's business" (Peak & Glensor, 2004, p. 98).

Total Quality Management
Criticisms against government services and their legitimacy sparked new debates in the field of public administration in 1960s. The introduction of new management styles influenced both the private and public sectors. Edward Deming's concept of "total quality management" became a popular response to the problems that government faced (Peak & Glensor, 2004). Total quality management focuses on customer needs along with the needs of the personnel servicing the customers. Managers should lead their agencies to improve the quality of services based on the predetermined vision and

mission of the agencies. Service outcomes should be evaluated consistently, and necessary alignments must be done (Sozer, 2002). More importantly, the problem solving process should include the participation and feedback from the customers and the personnel.

In this system, citizens are viewed as customers like in the private sector. Therefore, measurement of effectiveness and efficiency should be largely based on the citizens' satisfaction. In the early 1970s, police started considering citizens as customers of their services like other governmental agencies that adopted a customer oriented service mentality (Denhardt & Denhardt, 2000).

New Public Management
The "New Public Management" phenomenon also can be viewed as one of the underlying philosophies of community policing. Over the past two decades, it has influenced both the nation and the world (Hoggett, 1996). The basic premise of new public management is to utilize market mechanisms based on public-choice assumptions and perspectives (Hood, 1995). It is described as a shift from a hierarchical traditional management style to a decentralized, innovative management and problem solving model (Butterfield, Edwards, & Woodall, 2005). "Public managers have concentrated on accountability and high performance and have sought to restructure bureaucratic agencies, redefine organizational missions, streamline agency processes, and decentralize decision making" (Denhardt & Denhardt, 2000, p. 550).

According to this perspective, creating a new sense of community, which cares and steps up to seek solutions to its own problems, is an essential task just like it is in community policing. Denhardt & Denhardt (2000) illustrated this point:

> Recently, there has been a rebirth of interest in the idea of community and civility in America. Political leaders of both major political parties, scholars of different camps, best-selling writers and popular commentators not only agree that community in America has deteriorated, but acknowledge that we desperately need a renewed sense of community. Despite increasing diversity in America, or perhaps because of it, community is seen as a way of bringing about unity and synthesis. In public administration, the quest for

community has been reflected in the view that the role of government, especially local government, is indeed to help create and support community. (p. 552)

Community policing philosophy emerged almost simultaneously with other management philosophies in public administration. In terms of organizational change, most of its basic components are similar to those of total quality and new public management. For this reason, it might be appropriate to conclude that community policing is a reflection of new public administration trends in policing.

Community policing philosophy emerged almost simultaneously with other management philosophies in public administration. In terms of organizational change, most of its basic components are similar to those of total quality and new public management. For this reason, it might be appropriate to conclude that community policing is a reflection of new public administration trends in policing.

Definition of Community Policing

The literature on community policing illustrates a wide range of definitions for community policing. Mainly, it is viewed as a philosophy rather than a program by many scholars (Cordner, 1997; Greene & Mastrofski, 1988; Maguire & Katz, 2002; Wycoff, 1988).

Goldstein (1987) described it as decreased tensions between the police and the community, more effective use of police resources, increased quality in police services, effectiveness in dealing with community problems, higher job satisfaction of police participating in community policing programs, and greater accountability to the community. Carter and Sapp (1998) argue that " community policing is a proactive, decentralized approach, designed to reduce crime, disorder, and fear of crime, while also responding to the community's explicit needs and demands" (p. 58). Stevens (2003) contends that "Community policing is a preventive approach through an empowered problem-solving partnership of police and the community to control crime, reduce the fear of crime and enhance the life style experiences of all community constituents" (p.13).

Scholars argue that community policing has become a label for every new and pioneering strategy in American policing. In short, the definition of community policing differs according to the person's perception, and seems to include anything related to the community

(Bayley, 1998b). According to Wycoff (1988) " The term *community-oriented* suggests so much that is general and so little that is specific that it risks being a barrier rather than a bridge to discourse about developments in policing" (p. 103). Greene and Mastrofski (1988) noted that whether community policing represents something really new or just rhetoric describing traditional policing in a different way is a conundrum that needs to be unraveled. Friedmann (1990) contended that it might not be something different than traditional policing in the community after all (p. 84).

Despite the fact that there is no clear cut definition of community policing, scholars have provided a list of common elements that are found in any program that deals with community policing. The Community Policing Consortium [CPC] (1994) and several other researchers identified the necessary components that should be included in any program categorized as community policing instead of providing a single definition for it (Brown, 1989; Roth & Ryan, 2000; Skolnick & Bayley, 1988, Trojanowicz, 1994). Some of the most commonly listed components are:

- Permanent assignments of officers to specific duty assignments and often certain geographical areas.
- Implementing community based crime prevention techniques such as citizen education, neighborhood watches, and surveying citizens.
- Significant decentralization of authority and responsibility.
- Accountability of the police to each neighborhood.
- Partnerships with public and private institutions and agencies.
- Adaptation of a problem solving approach to the agency.

Maguire & Mastrofski (2000) contend that defining community policing by dividing it into series of categories or dimensions is a common strategy among scholars. None of these definitions is right or wrong; it is just an attempt to define a framework to this movement (p. 6). Among those definitions, it is noteworthy to illustrate Cordner's (1997) broader definition of community policing that is widely accepted (Colvin & Goh, 2006; Kappeler & Gaines, 2005; Maguire & Mastrofski, 2000; Smith, Novak & Frank, 2001; Walker & Katz, 2005). It embraces almost every aspect discussed in the literature.

Building upon Manning's (1984) construct of community policing which consists of four structures: ideological, programmatic, pragmatic, and organizational system, Cordner (1997) introduced four dimensions of community policing. The first one is the "philosophical dimension" which consists of three elements: citizen input, broad function, and personal service. These elements stress citizen input for police policies and community problems. Broad police function is based on the assumption that policing is not merely enforcing the law, but that there is more to policing than just enforcement. Order maintenance, social services, and enhancing quality of life measures are all in the scope of the broad police function. The personal service element refers to adjusting policing according to local norms and values as well as individual needs.

Cordner's second dimension of community policing is the "strategic dimension", which consists of three operational concepts: reoriented operations, prevention emphasis, and geographic focus. These concepts translate the philosophy into an action. By re-oriented operations, he refers to a shift from traditional strategies such as motorized patrol, rapid response, and detective investigations to a more proactive approach in which police focus more on preventing crime and targeting minor offenses and disorder. The concept of geographic focus requires permanent assignments of patrol officers in smaller areas. Officers are held responsible for incidents occurring in these smaller precincts, where they can have more face-to-face contact with citizens (Cordner, 1997).

The third dimension Cordner attributes to community policing is the "tactical dimension", which consists of three behavioral and tactical concepts: positive interaction, partnership, and problem solving. Officers should establish positive interaction with the community utilizing every means possible. Building trust, familiarity, and confidence are key factors to gain community participation in police activities. Police should facilitate community partnership by finding common interests aimed at people living in the same area. The third concept, problem solving, requires identifying conditions that cause crime, and solving those problems through citizen input within a broad range of solutions (Cordner, 1997).

The fourth dimension of community policing is the "organizational dimension", which has a crucial effect on implementation. This dimension also has three concepts: structure, management, and information. Police should restructure themselves to facilitate philosophical, strategic, and tactical dimensions. Police agencies should decentralize to provide service. Cordner (1997) highlights the necessity of reexamining the way employees are supervised and managed. The employees should be positively supervised by the values of the organizational culture. They should be encouraged to express their ideas and thoughts in a creative way to contribute to reaching the departmental goals (Cordner, 1997).

The concept of information focuses on police agencies' need to reconsider their information systems in terms of their support and usefulness for community policing. Police have to gather useful information about neighborhoods when implementing community policing. High- tech systems such as *Compstat* and *geographic information systems,* which empower police commanders to select the best tactics to solve neighborhood problems, are the most popular techniques currently used in major American cities (Walsh, 2005).

How does the researcher define community policing? Similar to the current trend of creating a definition by dividing community policing into dimensions or elements, each theory used in this book is considered an aspect of community policing. Thus, the definition will be that community policing is solving problems, fixing broken windows, strengthening community cohesion, and changing the management mentality and style. From each aspect, many elements and sub-elements can be created. As demonstrated, it is easy to create a wide scope definition of community policing; however, it is almost impractical to define community policing in a way that encompasses every activity implemented under its banner in each agency. Therefore, at the operational level, community policing is defined within the scope of items available in the LEMAS survey.

Major Objectives of Community Policing

Community policing is not just a program having a single unified form to implement. Rather, it varies according to the community and its needs along with the police department that attempts to apply it (Peak & Glensor, 2004, p. 64). In the United States, many programs have been established under the banner of community policing. Each program has had slightly different objectives to achieve; however, certain common strategies used in these programs distinguish a community policing strategy from traditional policing (Wycoff, 1988). For example, COPS (2000) developed four basic objectives to implement community policing: building partnerships with the community, problem solving, crime prevention, and organizational change. In the following section, current community policing programs will be discussed taking these objectives into account.

Community Partnership
The expression "community partnership" has dominated both private and public sector management ideology for at least the last three decades (Roth et al., 2004). The participation of citizens in solving community problems is essential in almost every community based program. Without community participation, any community policing program is subject to fail. Thus, community is an important element in a program's failures or successes (Vinzant & Crothers, 1994). Not surprisingly, the collaborative partnership between community and police is one of the major premises of community policing to improve police performance (MacDonald, 2002). Through two-way communication, police departments obtain more information regarding community needs, and they are able to generate appropriate responses by working closely with the community (CPC, 1994). Although police agencies use a variety of partnership tactics, Bayley (1996) and Roth et al. (2004) classified the tactics under two major categories with slight differences.

According to Bayley (1996), the first partnership category is *consultation.* This refers to defining and prioritizing neighborhood problems by reaching community residents. Police receive information about community problems including complaints about police, and they also have an opportunity to educate and inform community members about crime and disorder along with the department's success and failure. In this process, the two-way information flow makes the police and the residents co-producers of public safety (Greene, 2000). In addition to its contribution to public safety, receiving feedback from the community can be used in the performance appraisal of police officers, assessing the quality of police service, and in the police department's program evaluation (McGarrel, Benitez, & Gutierrez, 2003).

The second partnership category is *mobilization,* which refers to the active participation of community members and organizations in crime prevention strategies. The most common example of this strategy is "Neighborhood Watch" and "Crime Stoppers". When community members actively engage in crime prevention strategies, a sense of community and community cohesion are increased (Bayley, 1996). Police, in addition to community members, work closely with community organizations, businesses, and other agencies to improve the quality of life issues such as working with the municipality to remove graffiti, working with landlords to properly maintain property, and working with parks and recreation agencies to provide recreational programs for youths (Bayley, 1996).

Roth et al. (2004) categorized the types of partnership activities as *community partnership* and *problem solving partnership.* "The former varied from mere information sharing to coordination (i.e., planning and executing joint activities involving all partners) to occasional collaboration such as adaptation by all partners of a joint agenda" (p. 10). Advisory committees that utter public concerns to the police agencies are the most common examples of community partnership. The latter refers to solving community problems by working collaboratively with other service providers. Elected officials, school officials, and business representatives all take part in this partnership to improve the quality of life of the neighborhood.

Roth et al. (2004) explored the adoption efforts of community policing nationwide within a framework of the COPS office's four major objectives. They conducted multiple-wave surveys using a sample of small and large departments to determine implementation trends in community policing for the period of 1995 through 2000.

In terms of partnership building, Roth et al. found that "between 1995 and 1998, the growth in use of eight partnership tactics was statistically significant. In contrast, between 1998 and 2000 only the percentages of agencies conducting citizen police academies and crime prevention projects with businesses continued to grow slowly" (p.7). Another study examining changes in agencies' community partnership efforts between 1992 and 2002 found that volunteer citizen workers in agencies, citizen's patrols organized by agencies, and participation in citizen police academies increased significantly within ten years (Fridell & Wycoff, 2004).

Crime Prevention

Community policing refers to a major change in the role of police (Walker & Katz, 2005). Instead of emphasizing crime control, the role of police within community policing philosophy emphasizes partnership with the community in solving problems about which the community is most concerned (Palmiotto, 2000). This shift in the role of police attempts to accomplish a "crime prevention" goal rather than crime control (Riechers & Roberg, 1990).

The central tenets of community policing crime prevention have their roots in programs and studies in the 1970s (Rosenbaum, 1986). Programs like neighborhood watch, citizen patrols, increasing lighting, and target hardening were early examples, and they include tactics which can be still observed in today's crime prevention strategies. "Prevention has, in many ways, been the gateway to community policing, as many of the earliest collaborative interactions with the public have been for prevention" (Roth et al. 2004, p. 15). Community policing and problem solving (COPPS) are essentially about preventing crime and they are inextricably linked with each other. According to Peak and Glensor (2004), COPPS and crime prevention have six points in common: dealing with the health of community, addressing underlying causes and problems, dealing with the combination of physical and social issues that are at the center of many community problems, requiring active community participation, requiring participation beyond law enforcement, and being a philosophy rather than a program (pp. 99-100).

There are many programs available today under the rubric of crime prevention such as "National Night Out", "DARE", "McGruff", "Walk and Talk", "Cops and Cons", "Crime Stoppers", "Foot Beat", citizen patrols, and property identification projects. Although some of those programs neither include any community participation, nor target any underlying cause of problems (Greene & Taylor, 1988), they are consistently identified as community policing programs by practitioners (Roth et al. 2004).

Sherman and Eck (2006) argued that the crime prevention effects of community policing occur in four major ways. First there are watch programs, in which the residents keep their eyes on possible criminal activities in the community. Second, there is community-based intelligence, in which information flows from the community to the police. Third, police send more information to citizens regarding crime patterns and updated risks. Finally, police legitimacy, in which the public trust is gained for collaboration and fostering law abiding behavior among community members.

Sherman and Eck (2006) evaluated several studies examining the effect of community policing on crime prevention in terms of the four major ways that they are identified. They concluded that watch programs consistently showed no impact on crime. In addition, they assessed the impact of three popular programs intended to increase contact between police and citizens. The first program was *community meetings*, which were effective only if the meetings focus on specific crimes and their underlying problems. The second program was *door-to-door contacts*, which revealed moderately strong evidence of significant crime prevention (p. 317). The third program was *store fronts*, which were argued to be effective in certain areas with specific type of communities.

Like watch programs, the effect of information transmitted from police to citizens showed no significant impact on crime and victimization. Of the four major ways, police legitimacy had the greatest impact on crime and victimization consistent with the theory of "procedural justice". That is, if the citizens believe that the police represent legitimate legal authorities, they are more likely to cooperate and to obey the law (Tyler, 1990). "A consistent body of research shows that a key reason that adults support police is that they view police as legitimate" (Lyn, 2007, p. 206). As a final word, Sherman and Eck (2006) noted that any program that increases police legitimacy has the potential to prevent crime.

Roth et al. (2004) explored police departments' most common crime prevention strategies by conducting a survey. Survey findings revealed that agencies increasingly used crime prevention programs such as DARE, Boys and Girls Clubs, and other similar youth-police interaction programs along with foot and bike patrol. Based on their field observations, they reported that education about victimization avoidance, crime prevention tips via the internet, tenant screening, drug and gun hot lines, and safety planning were the most common crime prevention tactics used by the departments (p. 18).

Problem Solving

Goldstein (1977) argued that "the failure of team policing was due to a focus on secondary considerations" such as generating an organizational change without a clear focus on underlying problems creating calls for service (p. 238). Currently, community policing is viewed as the impetus for drastic changes in both organization and philosophy; therefore, team policing, at best, can be perceived as a partial reflection of current community policing (Hickman, Piquero, & Greene, 2000).

In his later work, Goldstein (1990) emphasized the importance of community collaboration while solving the underlying causes that were responsible for the calls for service. Yet some scholars prefer to distinguish community policing and problem-oriented policing (Eck & Spelman, 1987a; Sherman & Eck, 2006; Tilley, 2004; Walker & Katz, 2005). Those scholars suggest that the roots of community policing and problem solving are distinct. One of the main reasons that community policing emerged was that police were alienated from the community they served (Champion & Rush, 1997; Miller & Huss, 2002; Rosenbaum, 1988). On the other hand, a major impetus for problem solving was that police had failed to address chronic problems (Goldstein, 1990).

Second, what really differentiates those two are the ends over means syndrome. Problem-oriented policing stresses the importance of the final product rather than stressing the means by which policing is done (Eck & Spellman, 1987a). In community policing, the ultimate goal is to establish positive relations between police and the community. In problem-oriented policing, solving chronic problems that create calls for service is the primary goal. Unlike community policing, in problem solving, community involvement is not necessarily a prerequisite (Eck & Spellman, 1987b; Eck & Maguire, 2000; Sherman & Eck, 2006; Walker& Katz, 2005). Based on this perspective, it seems accurate that community involvement is secondary in the course of solving problems.

However, the relationship between community policing and problem solving is a dependent one. There has to be a geographic boundary and a community having special problems to be solved in order to implement problem-oriented policing that will effectively address local problems; and this can be best achieved with community involvement (Kelling & Moore, 1988). Moreover, community policing today not only offers legitimate relationships between the community and the agency, but it also offers tangible benefits such as crime prevention, and a reduction in disorder and fear of crime (Tilley, 2004).

Despite the fact that problem-oriented policing can be implemented alone or in conjunction with community policing, scholars and practitioners view problem solving as the core element of community policing (Bayley, 1994; COPS, 2000; Cordner, 1997; Hickman et al, 2000; Skogan, 2006; Stevens, 2003; Ortmeier, 2002). For example, in an assessment of the community policing program in Brooklyn, New York, officers declared that they viewed community policing as a valuable tool to identify community problems and to solve them in collaboration with community residents (Pate & Shtull, 1994). Community policing officers in St. Petersburg, Florida viewed reducing repeat calls for service as a more important goal than handling their call load or making arrests (Mastrofski, Parks, Reiss, Worden, 1999).

In short, community policing without a focus on solving the community's chronic problems is no different than traditional policing with extra attention focused on public relations. Therefore, community policing should not be viewed as a distinct phenomenon unlike problem-oriented policing. Rather, it should be viewed as a philosophy that emphasizes community participation in problem solving (Palmiotto, 2000).

Goldstein's (1979, 1990) problem-oriented policing philosophy has been put into practice in the form of the SARA model by most of the police departments in America (Kappeler & Gaines, 2005). SARA is a four stage process in problem solving, which refers to: scanning, analysis, response, and assessment (Eck & Spelman, 1987b).

Scanning is the first stage in identifying problems within the agency jurisdiction. Information on the identification of problems might come through different sources such as the officers' examination of intensive calls for service areas, a high volume of citizen complaints, and citizen feedback (Walker & Katz, 2005).

The analysis stage requires the agency to gather detailed information regarding the full scope of the problem. This includes the basic 5Ws and 1H questions (who, where, what, when, why and how) along with past responses by the community and its institutions (Eck & Spelman, 1987b).

In the response stage, based on data gathered in the early stages, the agency should develop a response that deals with the cause of the problem rather than its symptoms (Kappeler & Gaines, 2005). The response should cover all of the conditions that generate the problem. In some cases, other official and social agencies, local businesses, and any other community member or group might be needed to participate directly or indirectly in that process (Walker & Katz, 2005).

After the implementation has been completed, the agency must assess whether the treatment worked. The assessment stage should cover both the process and the impact evaluation. The former refers to the response that was implemented as planned, while the latter refers to examining the effectiveness of the response in achieving the expected results (Palmiotto, 2000).

Problem-oriented policing has been implemented in conjunction with other policing strategies such as hot spot and community policing in many jurisdictions (Eck & Spelman, 1987a in Newport News; Green, 1995 in Oakland; Mazerolle, Ready, Terrill, & Waring, 2000 in Jersey City; Pate & Skogan, 1985 in Newark). To identify those programs under the category of a specific policing strategy is difficult, yet the emphasis on problem solving components of the studies is more advanced than other policing strategies. It is evident that problem-oriented policing embraces a number of other strategies such as directed patrols, proactive arrests, and target hardening because each identified problem requires a specific response (Sherman & Eck, 2006). A single response extracted from a wide spectrum of policing strategies makes it difficult to classify the strategy specifically as "problem-oriented policing"; therefore, a general evaluation of problem-oriented policing is complicated in terms of disentangling other strategies from problem-oriented policing.

In an effort to evaluate problem-oriented policing, Sherman & Eck (2006) examined several studies' findings in terms of their ability to prevent crime. The crime prevention effect of problem-oriented policing occurs in two major forms: Eliminating the prerequisite of a crime, which refers to removing criminogenic elements (drugs, guns, alcohol) from the environment that facilitate the commission of a crime, and intercepting the convergence of offender and victim at the same time and place (p. 300). They reported that problem-oriented policing that focused on eliminating criminogenic elements consistently was found to be effective in preventing crime. Moreover, problem-oriented policing targeting problem places and applying appropriate strategies to eliminate the underlying causes of crime resulted in crime reduction in targeted areas (pp. 319-321).

"Since problem solving has been incorporated within community policing over the last decade, it has become even more common and accepted" (Cordner & Biebel, 2005, p. 177). However, the interpretation of problem solving varies in practice. Roth et al. (2004) used eleven tactics to examine the level of adaptation of a problem solving strategy in agencies. Nearly all of the agencies used at least three tactics, and community involvement was the most widely reported tactic to identify problems and assess the effectiveness of responses. A similar study by Fridell and Wycoff (2004) revealed that between 1992 and 2002, agencies participated in a survey that showed significant increases in six types of problem solving activities. "The largest increases were seen in citizen training in problem identification and resolution, landlord/manager training programs, the use of specialized problem-solving units, and interagency code enforcement" (p. 52).

Despite the fact that problem-oriented policing and community policing have different origins and philosophies, they are currently viewed and utilized as integrated strategies by the majority of agencies involved in preventing crime.

Organizational Change
Community policing cannot succeed without essential alterations inside the organization of police agencies (Redlinger, 1994). It not only requires a philosophical shift regarding police mission, but it also requires a commitment to alter the organization and the structure (Kappeler & Gaines, 2005). Eck and Maguire (2000) discuss the need for organizational changes in three areas: organizational structure, organizational culture, and management styles (pp. 217-223).

Organizational Structure
Traditional police organizations have a military type hierarchical system and management style, in which community policing cannot be achieved (Miller & Huss, 2000). "Community policing requires the shifting of initiative, decision making, and responsibility downward within the police organization" (CPC, 1994, p. 22). Community policing demands a flattened hierarchy giving beat officers more authority and flexibility to respond to community-specific problems. Parallel with changes in the private and public sector, police agencies within the frame of community policing should be more decentralized, and should empower beat officers to make decisions and participate in management (Mastrofski, 1999).

Another issue regarding the change in the organizational structure is assigning officers to certain geographic areas so that they can become familiar with their areas, their residents, and the area's specific problems. The hypothesis is that if an officer is assigned to a particular beat, he/she will respond more effectively to residents' concerns.

Moreover, officers can be held accountable for the incidents that take place in their beats, which, in turn, creates a sense of ownership in the assigned area among the officers.

Organizational Culture

The core elements of traditional policing such as crime fighting, quick response time, and making a large number of arrests are assumed by police cadets when they enter the police force. The tenets of traditional police culture resist change in the view of police officers (Walker & Katz, 2005). A study conducted by Zhao, Thurman, and Lovrich, (1995) revealed that the implementation of community policing in agencies was frustrated more by internal organizational barriers than obstacles in the community. Agencies which scored higher on internal resistance were less likely to implement community policing.

The changes in organizational structure, giving more authority to line officers, embracing line officers' input in department management, and modifying promotional standards regarding community policing activities might facilitate the process of cultural change in the organization (Glensor, Correia, & Peak, 2000). Agencies, in which organizational culture was modified successfully, had officers who were more likely to see both targeting minor offenses and disorder as real police work and assisting citizens as important as enforcing the law (Mastrofski et al., 1999). The modification of organizational culture distinguishes the type of activities in which officers engage. For example, one study revealed that community policing officers spent significantly more time on nontraditional police activities than beat officers, and beat officers spent significantly more time on traditional police activities than community policing officers (Smith et al., 2001).

However, efforts for changing organizational culture do not always produce the expected outcome. In a recent study which examined the differences between traditional and community policing agencies' performance evaluation criteria, it was found that the traditional agencies did not emphasize the enforcement role of officers significantly more than the community policing agencies. At the same time, the helping or service role of the officers in performance evaluations was not emphasized significantly more than in other agencies (Lilley & Hinduja, 2006, p. 506).

Management

The management style in community policing should also be different than in traditional policing. In traditional management, the primary concern is maintaining discipline by stressing departmental rules and regulations (Walker & Katz, 2005). However, police managers in community policing should assist line officers in developing community contacts and in finding resources to solve community problems. This task might be achieved by vertical staff meetings where line officers can discuss issues that emerged in the communities they serve with their supervisors (Kappeler & Gaines, 2005).

Community policing might enable supervisors to alter their management role. For example, middle managers in Indianapolis, Indiana perceived that helping officers to respond to community problems is more important than strictly enforcing departmental policies and procedures (Mastrofski, Parks, & Worden, 1998). In some agencies, community policing is implemented by the chiefs who would like to be seen as progressive and willing to enhance public relations despite the fact that they really do not believe in community policing principles. In fact, not many changes typically occur in these types of agencies. Community policing that is all about cosmetics and basic service delivery is still based on the traditional policing mentality (Hunter & Barker, 1993).

Another important issue regarding management is the role of the mid-level supervisors. In some cases, even though the police chief sincerely tries to change the organization in compliance with community policing philosophy, "middle managers, who have the responsibility to operationalize the goals and objectives of the chief executive fail to take an ownership role in implementing community policing" (Vito, Walsh, & Kunselman, 2005, p. 508).

Roth et al. (2004) measured the organizational change in agencies from 1995 to 2000. They used ten items to measure the organizational change such as mission and vision values, level of officer discretion, and revised evaluation criteria. They found that among the ten items, the most rapidly growing changes were: revised mission statement and performance criteria for community policing officers.

In their field observations, Roth et al. (2004) also noticed that police officers were given more time and discretion to perform community policing in their beats (pp. 23-24). Similarly, community policing agencies experienced the largest increase in the use of citizen surveys to evaluate police services, employee evaluations to reinforce community policing and problem solving, the physical decentralization of field services, and the use of fixed shifts from 1992 through 2002 (Fridell & Wycoff, 2004, p. 54).

Did the management style of community policing alter the basic functions of policing in the U.S.? In an attempt to answer this question, Zhao, He, and Lavorich, (2003) examined the 1990s by using three waves of panel data with regard to service priority changes in police agencies. They found that the crime control function still remained the top priority in agencies while the service provision was the lowest priority. Community policing, however, was a significant predictor of all the police functions. Agencies implementing community policing to a greater extent addressed all three core functions (crime control, order maintenance, and service provision) of policing successfully. Based on their findings, it is evident that police departments now implement more community policing activities. Nonetheless, a claim that community policing altered the service priorities drastically would be inaccurate.

It is obvious that community policing is a highly popular policy in American policing today. A majority of agencies throughout the nation have attempted to alter how they police their communities through community policing. "Does it work?" is a question yet to be answered satisfactorily. The next section reviews previous research on community policing and its relationship to crime.

CHAPTER 3

Community Policing and Crime Rates

Police can do little to control crime (Bayley, 1994). This view offers some support to criminological theories which contended that other factors generate crime and overshadow the role of police in dealing with crime. According to White (2007), not a single criminological theory discusses the potential capability of law enforcement agencies to solve or prevent crime. In fact, traditional policing can do little about the root causes of crime such as poverty, unemployment, child rearing, family structure, and gun and drug policies. On the other hand, community policing stresses the idea that police can prevent crime while enhancing their relationships with the communities they serve (Braga & Weisburd, 2006). Nevertheless, within the community policing context, police departments as a single agency cannot respond to all problems related to crime as it encompasses a variety of causes, factors, and correlates (Kappeler & Gaines, 2005). If this is the case, can community policing affect crime?

A single satisfactory answer about the impact of community policing on crime is not readily available as studies have demonstrated inconclusive results (Cordner, 1988, GAO, 2003, 2005; Mastrofski, 2006; MacDonald, 2002; Sherman & Eck, 2006; Police Foundation, 1981, 1984; Skogan, 2006; Weisburd & Eck, 2004; Zhao, Scheider, Thurman, 2002; Zhao & Thurman, 2004). Generally, community policing without a clear focus on specific problems has not been found to be effective in preventing crime. Similarly, it was found that foot patrols, storefront offices, newsletters, and community meetings do not reduce crime (Weisburd & Eck, 2004). Yet, these strategies have been found somewhat effective in reducing fear of crime and increasing citizen satisfaction with police services (Braga & Weisburd, 2006).

One possible explanation for the contradictory results in previous studies concerns validity issues such as the definition and construct problem of community policing (Lurigio & Rosenbaum, 1986). Some programs may have been identified as community policing when they really did not include the core elements of community policing philosophy (Greene & Mastrofski, 1988). In addition, for more than a decade, the nation has witnessed a crime drop, coinciding with the same time period when community policing was being increasingly adopted throughout the nation. Yet, an assessment of whether or not community policing has contributed to this crime reduction remains inconclusive (Eck & Maguire, 2000).

At the very least, community policing is deemed to be more effective in preventing and controlling crime than traditional policing due to the fact that the core elements of traditional policing are still visible in community policing agencies such as responding to calls for service, patrolling, and detectives' investigations. In short, community policing agencies simply do something more than the traditional policing agencies do (Kappeler & Gaines, 2005). It was also evident that studies indicating a reduction in crime were those that included a more complex variety of activities as a measure of community policing (Yin, 1986). Therefore, a closer examination of previous research might provide a clearer picture of what has been studied regarding community policing and crime thus far.

PREVIOUS RESEARCH

Oliver (2000) adapted a public policy theory (theory of innovation, diffusion, and institutionalization) to the community policing literature to provide the heuristic device to generate three distinct generations through which community policing has evolved. He briefly explains the theory:

> It essentially posits that most public policies are developed by specific political entities (e.g., states, counties, etc.) and that these policies then spread across other similar political entities. This process of diffusion moves public policy into a common state of being as

accepted practice among a majority of political entities. In other words, the policy becomes institutionalized. (p. 374)

Oliver's (2000) definition of "institutionalization" was used as a reference to distinguish previous research on the community policing and crime relationship. More specifically, previous research is examined in two phases: before and during the institutionalization phase. In the following section, a number of famous studies are reviewed. Then, findings of other studies conducted in this phase (prior to the institutionalization phase) are discussed.

Prior to Institutionalization Phase

In Flint, Michigan, a foot patrol program was implemented as a community policing program between 1979 and 1982. Although the program was called the Neighborhood Foot Patrol Program, it was more than just police walking on the streets. Community policing activities such as community involvement, two-way information flow between police and community members, recognition of specific neighborhood problems, and calls for other agencies to help neighborhoods to solve their problems were included among the patrol officers' tasks. The program was implemented in 14 experimental neighborhoods. At the initiation of the program, it was determined that 14 different neighborhoods would serve as control areas. In short, there were 28 neighborhoods in the study sample. However, because of the popularity of the program, the proposed control areas were also provided with foot patrol services, and the control group in this study became problematic (Trojanowicz, 1983). The researchers conducted interviews with residents and police officers, analyzed changes in official crime data, did a content analysis of local media, and monitored the extent and nature of foot patrol officers by sampling their daily, weekly, and monthly reports. Trojanowicz's (1983) findings regarding the program's impact on crime were encouraging. Crime was down in all categories except for burglary and robbery. In general, those two types of crime increased drastically for Flint, Michigan. Moreover, those two crimes primarily occurred at night, when foot patrols were not on the streets. Over the three years, crime in the 14 experimental areas decreased by 8.7%; whereas it increased 10% in the rest of Flint (Trojanowicz, 1983). Since foot patrol areas were not selected randomly, it was difficult to claim that the reduction in crime was solely due to the implementation of foot patrol. Furthermore, patrol beats were not comparable to control beats because they were not similarly matched on demographic characteristics. Lastly, no significance tests were reported; thus, the findings of the study should be interpreted cautiously (Sherman & Eck, 2006).

The New Jersey Safe and Clean Neighborhoods program was evaluated by the Police Foundation in 1981. A quasi experimental design was used in this study by creating three experimental conditions. The experiment phase occurred from February 1978 through January 1979. Of the eight beats which had had foot patrol since the program began, four sets of two beats were created. Among those pairs one discontinued foot patrol (Drop condition) while the other continued to have foot patrols (Retain condition). Additionally, foot patrol was instituted in four areas where it had not previously existed (Add condition) (Pate, 1986, pp. 140-142).

In this design, there were two potential threats to the accurate interpretation of results. First, there was the nonequivalence of treatment groups. That is, some beats had foot patrol before while some beats did not have it. Therefore, the difference in results between the two types of beats might have been due to the pre-test difference rather than due to the condition of the experiment. Second, in order to avoid the internal validity threat of "testing effect", researchers used different samples for the pre-test and post-test by matching them on a variety of characteristics. Other than those two threats, which the researchers recognized, the research was designed rigorously. The experimental process was also monitored carefully to validate that the treatment had been implemented as planned. Data were gathered from the residents of the beat through questionnaires administered before and after the experiment. Archival data, such as crime records, were used to test whether there was a change in recorded crime before and after the experiment (Pate, 1986, pp. 143-152).

The analysis performed by using beats as a unit of analysis revealed insignificant results, whereas analysis performed by using individuals as a unit of analysis yielded a number of significant results. Most of the results were based on survey responses of beat residents; consequently, the results reflected perceptions of the residents, rather than actual changes. In areas where foot patrol had only existed during the experiment period (add condition), residents' perceptions of severity of disorder and crime reduced significantly in comparison to the other two settings (retain and drop condition). In order to observe whether the program had any significant impact on crime rates, recorded crime rates before and after the program were also examined. "Based on this interrupted time series analysis, no significant differences across experimental conditions were found between the changes in levels or trends in recorded crime" (Pate, 1986, p. 152). The design of the Newark foot patrol evaluation was more rigorous than Flint's foot patrol evaluation. However, due to the threats to internal validity mentioned earlier, results of the Newark study should also be interpreted with caution.

The COPE (Citizens Oriented Police Enforcement) project was launched in 1982, in Baltimore County, Maryland. The initial focus of the project was to reduce fear of crime by utilizing saturated patrols and door to door visits for survey purposes. It later evolved into a combination of problem-oriented policing and community policing (Cordner, 1988). During the first phase, officers increased their contact with community members in targeted areas through foot patrols, door to door surveys, school programs, public meetings, and neighborhood watch programs. During the second and last phase, the police focused on gathering information about area-specific problems and developing responses to those problems. "COPE also began to rely less on traditional tactics, and to enlist the aid of more public and private agencies in their problem-solving efforts" (Cordner, 1988, p. 137).

For analysis purposes, pre and post tests were used without any specification of control groups. The lack of comparison groups created the potential for various internal validity threats such as history, testing, and selection. Another weakness of the evaluation was that most surveys were administered by the police officers, and this type of administration has raised questions about bias issues and the accuracy of the findings. Last, but not least, the impact of the program on crime was detected by comparing pre and post measures of reported crime to the agency. No other instruments, such as victimization surveys, were used to assess differences before and after the program.

Results indicated that during the first two years of the program, a reduction in target crimes occurred in 29 sites out of 37; and in five sites, crime remained unchanged. Finally an increase in crime was detected in only three cases (Cordner, 1988). In a separate analysis, 26 COPE sites were analyzed regarding all crimes (Part I and II) and calls for service from October 1983 through April 1985. Data were collected for three time periods: before the project, during the project, and after the project. The results revealed a 5% increase from before the project to during the project. However, there was a 12% decrease during the before project to after project period (Cordner, 1988, p. 142).

Programs which targeted the reduction of fear of crime in Newark and Houston were evaluated by the Police Foundation in 1984. The programs embraced a variety of community policing activities. They included community newsletters, community response teams, re-contacting victims, citizen contact patrols, reducing signs of crime, coordinated community policing, and police community stations (Pate, Wycoff, Skogan & Sherman, 1986). The declared objectives of these programs did not include reducing crime reported to the police; but, in Newark only, researchers examined change rates on recorded crime. Instead of examining other objectives of the program (perceived area physical deterioration, evaluation of police, and satisfaction with area), only results regarding crime (such as perceived area property crime, perceived area personal crime, and change in official crime rates) are reported in this book.

In each city, four experimental neighborhoods and one control area were selected carefully to match on certain demographic characteristics. Control areas had no new police programs. Program impacts were measured by a survey of residents before and after the programs were implemented. Programs began around September 1983 and were evaluated approximately ten months later. "In Newark, recorded crime data for Part I crimes were also collected for program and comparison areas, by month, from January 1980 through September 1984" (Pate, et al., 1986, p. 24).

First, pre and post survey results were analyzed together on a cross-sectional sample. In that design, the respondents of the pre-test and post-test were not the same residents (Pate et al., 1986) Consequently, the changes on outcome measures between pre and post tests might be attributable to the differences between respondents, not the changes in the perception of the same respondents over time.

Conversely, the second sample was a panel sample, in which respondents were the same people at both waves of the survey. In this design, the change over time for the same respondent could be detected since the pre-test was used as a statistical control in the analysis of the outcome measures. However, other threats to internal validity occurred in this case such as the attrition of respondents (not all subjects were retained for the second survey) and testing effect. Moreover, the post-test was conducted nearly ten months after the program started (Pate et al., 1986). The ten month time span might be insufficient to observe and evaluate the effects of programs on projected outcomes. Despite these limitations, this study was well designed and analyzed more rigorously than most evaluation studies on community policing.

Results revealed that the community newsletter and re-contacting victims in both Houston and Newark did not have any impact on perceived personal and property crime or on the recorded crime. Citizen contact patrols were found effective in reducing perceived personal and property crime in only the cross-sectional analyses, but not in the panel regression analyses. Police community stations in Houston were found effective in reducing perceived personal crime in both analyses; whereas, they were found effective in reducing perceived property crime only in the cross- sectional design. Like newsletters, re-contacting victims in Houston and "reducing signs of crime" in Newark did not yield any significant effect. However, in Newark, an interrupted time series analysis was conducted to examine whether recorded crime differed before and after the program. The analysis revealed that total Part I crimes, personal crimes, and burglary decreased significantly in the program area while there was no significant reduction in the control area (Pate et al., 1986, pp. 31-34).

Evaluation studies produced mixed results during the innovation and diffusion phases (from 1979-1994). While some studies illustrated that community policing had a positive impact on reducing crime in Seattle (Lindsey & McGill's, 1986), Portland (Schneider, 1978), Houston (Skogan & Wycoff, 1986), and Denver (Tien & Cahn, 1986), other studies had inconclusive results that varied based on the category of crime like Madison (Wycoff & Skogan, 1993) or type of community policing activities like Birmingham and Oakland (Uchida, Forst, Annan, 1992). It is also intresting to note that some studies found no effect like Minneapolis (Pate, McPherson, Silloway, 1987), Houston (Kessler & Duncan, 1996), and Boston (Bowers & Hirsch, 1987). Even though it was rare, only two studies revealed an increase in crime like Hartford (Fowler, McCalla, & Mangione, 1979), and St. Louis (Tien & Cahn, 1986).

Overall, during the innovation and diffusion phases (from 1979-1994), community policing was implemented in a number of large cities through testing and pilot studies (Oliver, 2000). Thus, evaluations were limited to individual programs in those few cities, and small departments were wholly ignored (Zhao et al. 2002). The individual programs, by and large, focused on a single method of community policing; and evaluations were based on case studies, or pre and post-test surveys either with or without comparison groups. The level of analysis was mostly individual level instead of community level in contrast to the underlying rationale for community policing (Greene & Taylor, 1988). The big picture of community policing in terms of both variety of activities and its effect on aggravate level was rarely examined (MacDonald, 2002). Therefore, the need for further studies and research persisted.

Institutionalization Phase

After the enactment of the Violent Crime Control and Law Enforcement Act of 1994 (the beginning of institutionalization phase), community policing was adopted throughout the nation. This enabled large spectrum studies to be conducted (Rosenbaum, 1994). The government appropriated $8.8 billion to law enforcement agencies through COPS funding; and the money was to be utilized for hiring, equipping, and training police officers according to the community-policing philosophy (Oliver, 2000). The amount of money allocated for community policing programs was unprecedented. As a result, the government and scholars were determined to assess whether community policing works. During the 'institution' phase (from 1994 to present), both specific case studies and aggregate level studies have been conducted by researchers on the different objectives of community policing such as organizational change (Lilley & Hinduja, 2006; Pate & Shtull, 1994; Ren, Cao, Lovrich, & Gaffney, 2005; Redlinger, 1994; Smith et al., 2001; Vito et al., 2005; Zhao et al., 1995), change in officers' and citizens' roles (Hickman et al., 2000; Mastrofski et al., 1999; Reisig, 2002; Reisig & Parks, 2004; Vinzant & Crothers, 1994), and effectiveness in preventing crime and reducing the fear of crime (Davis & Maxwell, 2003; Giacomazzi & McGarrell, 2002; Kelling & Sousa, 2001; Robert & Maxwell, 2003; Robert & Taylor, 1997; Rooh & Oliver, 2005; Skogan, 2006). This section focuses on the aggregate level studies examining the crime-community policing relationship.

Zhao et al. (2002) examined the effect of COPS funding awarded between 1994 and 1998 on official crime rates in 6,100 U.S. cities between 1995 and 1999. They specifically considered three types of COPS grants: Making Officer Deployment Effective (MORE), innovative grants, and hiring grants. Mostly, COPS' funds were targeted to provide money for hiring new officers; therefore, the most obvious result of these grants was an increase in the number of police officers.

The study was designed to test whether there was a change in crime rates due to the COPS grants. Zhao et al. (2002) used UCR property and violent crime data from 1994 to 1999. The second source of data was the amount of money provided by the COPS office; the amount of money was standardized by dividing the total amount of dollars by 100,000 residents. The third source of data was the 1990 U.S Census Data. The fourth data set gathered unemployment data from the Bureau of Labor Statistics. The unemployment rate and census variables served as control variables.

Zhao et al. (2002) used a two factor- fixed effect model to observe the impact of funding on a change in crime rates. Two factors (place and time) which might have affected crime rates nationally were controlled by creating a binary indicator (dummy variable). The researchers looked at the influence of funding on property and violent crime separately for small cities (with a population less than 10,000) and large cities (with a population of more than 10,000). Results indicated that hiring and innovative grants had a significant negative effect on both violent and property crime rates in large cities. On the other hand, hiring grants had a significant positive effect on changes in crime rates in small cities. MORE and innovative grants had no effect on changes in crime in small cities. Analysis of the full sample (large and small cities) revealed that innovative grants had significant negative effects on both violent and property crimes. More specifically, a one dollar increase in innovative grant funding contributed to a decline of 12.26 violent and 43.85 property crime incidents per 100,000 residents.

In 2003, the Government Accountability Office asserted that Zhao et al. in their 2001 study omitted important variables, misspecified the model, and used a limited sample. More specifically, GAO suggested that other funds different than COPS funds coupled with state and local expenditures must have been controlled since the COPS program supports only a portion of agency budgets (p. 6). Moreover, the GAO contended that unmeasured variability would have been controlled at the city level instead of county level. The exclusion of state and county police agencies, sheriffs' offices, campus police, and special purpose law enforcement agencies was not appropriate because 40% of the COPS recipients consisted of such agencies. It should be noted that census variables used in this study are from 1990. The results must be evaluated with caution because many of the social factors which had an impact on crime rates might have undergone some change during this ten year period.

Based on GAO's criticism (2003), Zhao and Thurman (2004) revised their study by including one more year of data and by using Census data for the year 2000 instead of 1990. They also utilized city level dichotomous variables to control unmeasured variability across places and over time instead of county level dichotomous variables. Nevertheless, their findings did not change drastically. Overall Zhao and Thurman (2004) concluded that COPS funds had a substantial impact on crime for cities with a population over 10,000.

In contrast to the findings of Zhao et al. (2002, 2004) and the GAO (2003) studies, Muhlhausen (2001), in his county level analysis, found that COPS funds did not have any impact on violent crime. He criticized the methodological drawbacks of previous studies. Muhlhausen (2001) suggested that socioeconomic factors, and other criminal justice policies such as sentencing policies, incarceration rates, and the likelihood of going to prison due to the commission of a violent crime may also affect crime rates. Hence, the results of studies excluding those factors in their analysis should be interpreted with caution. Moreover, another challenge was levied against the assertion about the effectiveness of COPS grants. Nationwide, crime rates tended to decline (beginning in 1991) before COPS grants were ever made available to the agencies (GAO, 2003; Eck & Maguire, 2000).

In order to clarify the ongoing discussion about the effectiveness of COPS grants, the GAO (2005) conducted a comprehensive independent study on the nationwide effect of COPS funds. The GAO researchers used 12 years of data covering the years 1990 through 2001 for slightly over 11,000 agencies that reported at least one complete year of crime data to the FBI's Uniform Crime Reporting program. They obtained information on COPS grant expenditures from the Office of Justice Programs (OJP), financial data, county level income and employment data from the Bureau of Economic Analysis, and population totals and population breakdowns by gender, race, and age from the U.S Census Bureau. They linked all these data sets to each other, and generated a sample of 4,509 agencies with a population of 10,000 or more for an analysis of the impact of COPS expenditures on crime. The analysis focused on COPS funds' effects on changes in the number of officers; i.e., an increase in the number of police officers.

The GAO researchers employed population-weighted regression (crime rates on COPS funds and officer rates on COPS funds) by controlling social, ecological, and economical factors. They controlled for 880 variables, and then employed state by year fixed effects to control for the unmeasured state level sources of variation with crime. These included increases in state incarceration rates, changes in state sentencing practices, and changes in other state programs that could affect crime rates. They then estimated the effects of a one percent change on the level of sworn officers per capita on per capita crime rate. They attempted to estimate the reduction in crime nationally that could be attributable to COPS funds.

Results indicated that an increase in the number of sworn officers was associated with a reduction in crime rates. A one percent increase in the level of sworn officers per capita reduced robbery rates by 2%, aggravated assault rates by 0.5%, and larceny rates by 0.1%. The overall effect of a COPS grant on crime rates varied by the year and the level of COPS' grant expenditures. In 1998, COPS grant expenditures were related to 8% of the total decline in index crimes and about 13% of the total decline in the violent crime rate from its 1993 level. From 1999 through 2000, crime continued to decline. The COPS' grant was associated with 5% of the total reduction in index crimes and about 10% of the total reduction in violent crimes from their 1993 levels.

MacDonald (2002) examined the effectiveness of community and the problem solving policing efforts on the control of two violent crimes (robbery and homicide) in 164 major U.S. cities. These cities had a population over 100,000 according to 1990 U.S Census data. He hypothesized that, "if the community policing efforts that have been adopted in major American cities are effective at controlling violent crime, then cities that engage in more of these efforts should have lower rates of these criminal events" MacDonald, 2002, p. 600). Three data sources were used to test this hypothesis: the LEMAS survey data for the years 1993 and 1997 measured departmental factors related to community and problem solving policing; the 1990 U.S. Census data measured city level social ecological factors that are correlates of crime; and the UCR data computed city-level measures of violent crime rates for the years 1993, 1994, 1997, and 1998.

As predictor variables, community policing activities of agencies were measured by creating two measurements from the LEMAS survey data. The first one was a binary indicator variable indicating whether or not an agency had a community policing plan. The second was a summated index of five different variables related to community policing and problem solving (MacDonald, 2002). Moreover, departmental factors such as a composite index of special units, a dichotomous variable indicating the presence of police officers residing within a municipality, a proxy measure of aggressive policing, and an education requirement for new recruits were also included in the model. In order to control social ecological factors, the following variables were used: percentages of divorced males, single-parent households, population size, population density, percentage of people between the ages of 18 and 24, and income inequality.

Ordinary least square analysis was employed to test the effect of community policing on robbery and homicide rates. Two models were created to estimate the change in violent crimes from 1993 to 1994 and 1997 to 1998. Like Zhao et al.'s (2002) study, in order to control the influence of unmeasured variables, "fixed effect" estimation was used for the period from 1997 to 1998. Because this method was not able to detect the influence of independent variables that were constant over time (social ecological factors), a random effects model was also employed (MacDonald, 2002).

In 1997 and 1998, when the community and problem-solving training and practices were in operation, data indicated that aggressive enforcement had a significant negative effect on robbery, but not on the homicide rate. Conversely, community policing had no effect on robbery or homicide rates. The percentage of female households had a strong positive relationship with robbery and homicide rates; and the percentage of divorced males had a significant positive effect on the homicide rate. Results revealed that community policing plans and community and problem-solving training and practices had no effect on robbery or homicide rates over time. However, divorced men and female heads of households showed significant increases in robbery and homicide rates over time. A higher level of educational attainment had a negative impact on robbery while increases in the number of specialized units had a negative impact on homicide rate (MacDonald, 2002).

MacDonald's study did not totally control changes in social ecological factors over time across various places. He utilized 1990 Census data to control for social ecological factors when he analyzed the impact of community policing on crime rates from the years 1993 to 1999. It was likely that social ecological factors in 1990 were quite different than social ecological factors in 1999. However, this limitation is very common in aggregate level studies. In addition, he used a few community-policing and problem-oriented policing variables readily available in LEMAS survey. Even though LEMAS (1993) did not have questions regarding community policing activities, large departments were likely to start implementation of community policing activities before 1993.

As Oliver (2000) noted, during the diffusion period of community policing (1987-1994), especially large agencies instituted community policing activities. Therefore, a lack of any community policing effect might be due to the fact that there was really no change in those departments' community-policing plan and problem-oriented policing training and practices. However, with the available data, this study was an essential step in national level research on the effect of community policing.

To date, aggregate level studies have produced inconclusive results. Studies examining the impact of COPS grants on crime revealed that the nation witnessed a drop in crime due to federal grants allocated for community policing practices coupled with a greater number of police officers on streets (GAO, 2003, 2005; Zhao et al, 2002; Zhao & Thurman, 2004). Unfortunately, these studies do not examine any type of community policing activities. It is also difficult to find a clear indication of implementation because operationalization of community policing depended on a dichotomous variable. Instead, they simply focused on the changes in crime rates of the agencies which received funds from the COPS office. Some agencies appeared to be implementing community policing just to receive grant money from the federal government without making changes in the organization and operations (Lurigio & Rosenbaum, 1994). In order to observe whether community policing has an impact on crime, it is necessary to have some evidence indicating the implementation of community policing.

Aggregate level studies demonstrate somewhat the extent of implementation of community policing in departments. However, these studies failed to find a significant relationship between community policing and crime (Beckman, 2006; MacDonald, 2002). More importantly, they totally excluded small departments in their analyses, and limited the generalizibility of their findings to urban America. Weisheit (1993) characterized this as "urban ethnocentrism".

Large versus Small Departments

Community policing was the impetus for the changes that took place in American policing. It has long been established that police alone cannot solve crime problems. Community support is necessary to overcome area specific problems, and it is essential in every department regardless of its size (Benedict, Bower, Brown, & Cuningham, 1999). Nonetheless, aggregate level studies which examine the effect of community policing on crime rates tend to ignore small departments (Beckman, 2006; MacDonald, 2002).

Overlooking small agencies may mislead researchers in two ways. First, they will miss the natural laboratory of community policing as these officers generally know the service recipients personally, have face-to-face contact, and are involved in many activities different than traditional policing (Weisheit, Wells, & Falcone, 1994). Second, although crime rates are more likely to be lower in small jurisdictions, they are not evenly distributed across all small jurisdictions. Therefore, a conclusion that indicates crime rates and social factors do not vary across small agencies is likely to be inaccurate. Wells and Weisheit (2004) stated that "of the 30 counties with the highest homicide rates, 17 were non-metropolitan. Of these 17 non-metropolitan counties, 9 were completely rural; that is, the county contained no municipality of 2,500 or more. Of the remaining 8 non-metropolitan counties, 7 had no municipality over 20,000" (p. 2).

Social disorganization theory is applied to urban communities and largely ignored in rural and suburban settings. This does not mean that demographic factors that are well known correlates of crime and disorder are constant across rural and suburban settings (Osgood & Chambers, 2000). A study conducted by Wells & Weisheit (2004) found that the key contextual variables (poverty, family type, housing, race, and age dispersion) varied drastically even among most rural areas. Furthermore, the magnitude and the direction of impact of contextual variables on crime also differed in urban and rural settings. For example, one of the possible explanations of the reduction in crime during the 1990s was attributed to economic growth (Blumstein &

Wallman, 2000). By contrast, it was observed that economic growth was associated with an increase in crime rates in rural settings (Wells & Weisheit, 2004).

In fact, there are also some differences between large and small departments' police officers. Officers in large departments are less respected and supported by citizens than officers in small departments; and large departments' officers are less responsive to the community needs. According to Weisheit et al. (1994), officers in large departments are more responsive toward their departments' needs and dynamics. In that sense, small departments are deemed to experience the more positive effects of community policing.

Differences aside, similarities between the large and small departments also call for the inclusion of small departments in the analysis. A city-specific study in Choteau, Oklahoma with a population of 1,500 residents revealed parallel findings with its large city counterparts. After implementation of community policing in the area, citizens' perceptions of the police department, the quality of police services, safety, and crime improved significantly (Brand & Birzer, 2003). These data suggest that community policing does matter even in a very small rural area where researchers do not expect substantial variation in crime rates traditionally. Based on this finding, expecting an improvement as a result of community policing in small departments merits attention.

Another similarity between small and large departments is the focus on public safety. For example, 84% of 207 small departments in a sample study ranked property crimes at the top of the list just as their larger counterparts did, and ranked violent crime against individuals fifth among 17 types of crime on the list (GAO, 1995). If the goal is to prevent and control crime by establishing quality relationships between the community and police, community policing in small departments is as popular as it is in large departments (Zhao & Thurman, 2003).

Since community policing aimed to eliminate police–community alienation in urban settings, it was initially implemented in large cities and spread from city to city. Small cities lagged behind their larger counterparts in terms of adopting community policing. Nonetheless, support for community policing is widespread (Cordner & Scarborough, 2003; Hawkins & Weisheit, 2003; Zhao & Thurman, 2003). Between 1998 and 2000, smaller departments significantly increased their community policing activities (Roth et al., 2004). Furthermore, COPS grants entitled "Funding Accelerated for Smaller

Towns" (FAST), allocated resources especially for departments serving a population of fewer than 50,000. The creation of such funds also encouraged small departments to engage in community policing. In particular, jurisdictions with more reported crime were more likely to apply for this grant (GAO, 1995).

In their study of the impact of COPS funds on crime, Zhao et al. (2002) concluded that " the crime drop in America was not a unitary phenomenon in light of the different effects found in large versus smaller cities" (p. 28). Based on the results of previous studies, it appears that more recent studies should incorporate small departments in their analysis.

Nevertheless, it is noteworthy to carefully consider the extent of implementation of community policing in small departments. Although scholars posit that small departments embody community policing, it must not be assumed that they will systematically engage in community policing activities. One study found that even though more than half of the agencies in the study sample had a community policing program, few of them experienced internal and external organization change (Hawkins & Weisheit, 2003, p. 26).

The level of implementation plays an important role in determining whether community policing has an impact on crime. This statement lies at the core of the study presented in this book. Consequently, it is critically important to capture the measure of level of implementation rigorously unlike the studies which used dichotomous variables or which limited the number of variables used just to indicate the presence of community policing. Finally, this book is also unique because it examines the suburban and rural contexts as well as the urban one.

CHAPTER 4

Roadmap to Research

The purpose of this book is to assess the impact of community policing practices on crime rates. Previous studies that examined the relationship between community policing and crime trends yielded inconclusive results (Beckman, 2006; GAO, 2003, 2005; MacDonald, 2002, Muhlhausen, 2001; Zhao et al., 2002, Zhao & Thurman, 2004). However, none of those studies scrutinized the impact of community policing by considering various community policing practices across a variety of jurisdictions and organizational contexts at the same time. To overcome this shortcoming, the present book provides a more comprehensive national picture of the impact of community policing on crime by examining different organizational contexts and various community policing practices.

Experimental research is viewed as being superior to non-experimental research in terms of constructing causality, but non-experimental research can be a very effective tool for exploring the context in which causal effects occur (Bachman & Schutt, 2001, p. 165). Employing surveys and gathering archival data are more feasible than administering various experiments in different settings. In particular, administering experiments at the national level is an almost insurmountable project. This book utilizes three major data sets: LEMAS 2003, two waves of UCR data (2004 & 2005), and the 2000 U.S Census data to examine the relationship between community policing and crime at the national level.

Since this book utilizes cross sectional design, the intent is not to establish causation between community policing and crime, but rather to examine the relationship between them. The cross-sectional design enables the researcher to identify an association between two variables. However, it is difficult to establish time order with a cross-sectional design (Kraska & Neuman, 2007).

Bachman & Schutt (2001) contended that if the independent variables are fixed at some point prior to the variation in the dependent variable, cross-sectional data can be used to construct the time order of effects (p. 169). In spite of being cross-sectional, this book features a reasonable time order. The LEMAS survey asked the respondents to use June 30, 2003 as a reference date. For example, "During the 12-month period ending June 30, 2003, what proportion of agency personnel received at least eight hours of community policing training (problem solving, SARA, community partnerships, etc.)?" Thus, the agency responded to the question by considering activities from June 2002 to June 2003. The UCR data cover the crime rates from January to December of the years 2004 and 2005. Therefore, the utilization of the average of crime rates for the year 2004 and 2005 provides a time order in which independent variables precede dependent variables. Mernard (2002) defined this type of design as "time-ordered cross-sectional design" in which the independent variable is measured at some time before the dependent variable. Nevertheless, Mernard (2002) advised that one should be cautious about a risk of undetectable misspecifications due to incorrect casual order (pp. 25-26).

Research Questions and Hypotheses

Since 1993, crime in America has consistently declined (FBI, 2007). It is difficult to stipulate the net contribution of community policing to this decline simply because other social indicators such as economic growth and high employment also occurred during the 1990s (Blumstein & Wallman, 2000; Eck & Maguire, 2000; Lafree, 1998). In an attempt to examine this issue the first research question is as follows:

Does the level of implementation of community policing affect crime rates?

Earlier studies sought to answer this question (GAO, 2003, 2005; Muhlhausen, 2001; Zhao et al, 2002, Zhao & Thurman, 2004). However, in all of these studies a dichotomous (binary indicator) variable was utilized to operationalize community policing. The only criterion that indicates an agency implemented community policing was whether the agency got funded by the COPS office. Eck & Maguire (2000) argued that "policing is replete with superficial adoption of carefully crafted programs, so simply counting the number of agencies that claim to be using community policing is a poor indicator of the diffusion of the innovation" (p. 245). In agreement with their argument, this book employs scales to operationalize community policing. Thus, the construct of community policing is captured more precisely than previous studies. The related hypotheses are stated below:

Hypothesis 1 **If the level of implementation of community policing practices increases then the property crime rates will decrease.**

Hypothesis 2 **If the implementation of community policing practices increases then the violent crime rates will decrease.**

Hypothesis 3 **If the implementation of community policing practices increases then the total crime rate will decrease.**

This book is a departure from previous studies because it looks at the influence of community policing practices on both small and large agencies. It should be noted that there may be differences in the effect of community policing between large and small agencies. In order to address this issue, the following research question is added to this book:

Is there a difference between small and large agencies in terms of the effect of community policing on crime rates?

Although the focus of community policing is on urban neighborhoods that are deteriorated by poverty, disrupted families, and unemployed individuals (Robinson, Scaglion, & Olivero, 1994), those are the neighborhoods where community policing is less likely to be successful (Reisig & Parks, 2004). In small cities and towns, community partnership is an integral component of policing since officers are more likely to personally know residents of the community and to have more frequent face-to-face contact with them (Weisheit et al., 1994). Those small jurisdictions also have stronger social bonds and the neighborhoods are less likely to be demoralized. It might be the case that community policing is more likely to work in small jurisdictions. In order to address this issue, the following hypotheses will be tested.

> **Hypothesis 4: There is a difference between the small and the large agencies in terms of the impact of community policing on property crime rates.**
>
> **Hypothesis 5: There is a difference between the small and the large agencies in terms of the impact community policing on violent crime rates.**
>
> **Hypothesis 6: There is a difference between the small and the large agencies in terms of the impact of community policing on total crime rates.**

Uniform Crime Reporting Program Data

The UCR data have been gathered by the FBI since 1930 from city, county and state law enforcement agencies on a monthly basis. Although participation in the program is voluntary, the number of police departments and the comprehensiveness of reports have continually improved over the years. The UCR is composed of Part I and Part II crimes. In this book, Part I crimes were used because they are the crimes most likely to be reported and most likely to occur with sufficient frequency to provide an adequate basis for comparison. (FBI, 2004, p. 16). Offenses which constitute Part I crimes (Index Crimes) include murder, non-negligent manslaughter, forcible rape, robbery, aggravated assault, burglary, larceny-theft, and motor-vehicle theft (FBI, 2004, p. 20).

The UCR data have several limitations. First, they encompass only the crimes reported to the police. Hart and Rennison (2003) argued that less than half of the violent crimes and only one-third of the property crimes are reported to the police. Second, some agencies underreport the actual crimes that occurred within their jurisdictions because of political or performance related concerns (Bennett & Weigant, 1994; Ellis & Walsh, 2007). Third, despite the fact that FBI provides a guideline for classifying offenses based on pre-determined definitions, there might be a risk that the interpretation of an offense might differ from one agency to another (Kessler & Duncan, 1996).

Nevertheless, Kennedy & Veitch (1997) argued that what goes unreported are either those acts that citizens find not worth reporting because the harm inflicted is not significant or acts that do not fit the legal definition to be classified as crime by the police (p. 54). In addition, compared to victim surveys, UCR data are more likely to accurately reflect what is deemed a significant threat to the social order in the eyes of both police and citizens. Therefore, the UCR constitutes a valid measure of the extent of serious crime that exists (Kennedy & Veitch, 1997, Marvell & Moody, 1996).

LEMAS 2003 Sample Survey of Law Enforcement Agencies

The LEMAS survey data are gathered from a nationally representative sample of publicly funded state and local law enforcement agencies in the United States (Bureau of Justice Statistics [BJS], 2006, p. 4). "Topics covered include agency personnel, expenditures and pay, operations, community policing initiatives, equipment, and computerization" (Reaves & Hickman, 2005, p. 60). The LEMAS survey has been conducted since 1987 in three year intervals.

Within the large sampling frame, agencies were divided into two major categories: First, all agencies with 100 or more sworn officers were included in the sample as self-representing agencies. Second, a nationally representative sample of agencies with fewer than 100 sworn officers was drawn using a stratified random sampling technique, and they are categorized as non-self-representing agencies. Consequently, the final product consists of all agencies in the U.S having 100 or more sworn officers, and a sample of the remaining agencies. For each three year data wave, agencies included in the sample of non-self representing agencies differ.

The LEMAS 2003 survey was mailed to 3,154 agencies. A total of 2,859 agencies responded to the survey, which is a 90.6 % response rate. The final distribution of the sample in terms of agency type is: 863 sheriffs, 1,947 local police, and 49 primary state police. The total sample consists of 904 self-representing and 1,955 non-self-representing agencies (BJS, 2006).

The U.S Census 2000 Data

The Census 2000 Data are the latest official population census of the United States which is conducted every ten years. During each decennial census, the United States Census Bureau collects data from every household in the United States and its territories. It includes a wide variety of demographic information. The Census 2000 data contain information about 115.9 million housing units and 281.4 million people across the United States (U.S. Census Bureau, 2001). City level structural factors that are known as correlates of crime will be drawn from Census 2000 data, and were used as control variables in this book.

Law Enforcement Agency Identifiers Crosswalk 2000

Although UCR and LEMAS data can be linked at the county level, it is very difficult to merge two data sets at the city or place level. "To overcome this obstacle, BJS and the National Archive of Criminal Justice Data (NACJD) have created the Crosswalk, a file that lists agencies by the FBI's codes as well as other major identifying standards in use today" (Lindgren & Zawitz, 2001, p. 1). The main variables in Crosswalk enable researchers to take police agency-level data, combine them with the Census and LEMAS data, and perform place-level, jurisdiction-level, and government-level analyses.

Data Merging and Sample

The data sets to be used in this book do not have a common identifier that enables the researcher to merge them and create a combined data set at the place (jurisdiction) level. The Crosswalk 2000 data file has the common identifiers that was used to link these three data sets. First, the LEMAS 2003 data set was linked to Crosswalk 2000 by using the common identifier variable "agency ID". Second, the combined Crosswalk 2000 and LEMAS 2003 data sets were linked to Census 2000 through Federal Information Processing Standard (FIPS) codes that indicate state, county, city, and place location. Finally, UCR 2003 was merged to this combined data via Originating Agency Identifier (ORI7).

"In the simplest situation an agency appears in both the Census of State and Local Law Enforcement Agencies (CSLLEA) and the UCR system; it serves one geographic location; that location has an incorporated government; and UCR and FIPS codes are available. Many situations are not this simple" (Lindgren & Zawitz, 2001, p. 6). For example, since a university police department has the same city code with the city police department, both these agencies correspond to the same census variables which make utilization of structural control variables problematic. These kinds of problems are valid for all primary state police and *special-function departments* such as tribal, college/university, and airport police. Therefore, all primary state and special function police departments were excluded from the sample.

Some cases were lost during the data merging process. Even though Crosswalk 2000 provides the best possible common identifiers among these three data sets, the identifier variables in Crosswalk 2000 have several missing values. The primary reason for those missing values is that the source data files, mainly the UCR ORI file and the CSLLEA, do not correspond completely. Second, county codes and metropolitan statistical areas may change over time even though such occurrences are rare. As a result, losing several departments during the merging process was inevitable.

The Variables

The variables used in this book can be classified into three main groups: the dependent variables, the explanatory variables, and the control variables. The control variables are also classified into two groups as departmental and contextual (structural level) control variables.

The Dependent Variables

Part I crimes were used as dependent variables to test the hypotheses. The FBI's classifications for property and violent crimes were used to generate property, violent, and total crime rates. In the FBI classification; *violent crimes* include murder, non-negligent manslaughter, forcible rape, robbery, and aggravated assault, and *property crimes* include burglary, larceny-theft, and motor-vehicle theft (FBI, 2004). The effects of community policing practices on crime rates was explored by separately regressing community policing variables on the property, violent, and total crimes rates.

Sacco (2005) contends that the collection of UCR data can be viewed as a social constructionist process which is influenced by four major factors:

- Change in the definition of crime and its classification over time
- Individual tolerance that might differ with respect to how severe an offense must be worth to report it to police
- Bookkeeping quality which refers to unintentional errors during the data collection process
- Intentional manipulation of the records for the sake of the organization's legitimacy, performance, and reputation (pp. 67-72).

Due to these factors which might create possible variation in data recording practices, the two year (2004-2005) average rates were utilized to stabilize the variations and increase the efficiency of the estimates (MacDonald, 2002, p. 601).

Despite the limitations of the UCR data discussed above, they are the best measure of reported crime available at the national level (Zawitz et al., 1993). It is also argued that they are a fairly good measure of the more serious crimes within each crime category (Marvell & Moody, 1996).

To control for the population size, crime rates per 1,000 residents were used. There are three ratio level dependent variables (property crime rates per 1,000, violent crime rates per 1,000, and total crime rates per 1,000).

The Independent Variables

The "Community policing section" of LEMAS 2003 consists of 43 items which were used to operationalize community policing. Although all of the items in LEMAS 2003 are conceptually related to community policing, it is important to determine the factors that underlie those items. In the case of 43 items, factor analysis can be used to determine whether one broad or several more specific constructs are needed to characterize the item set (DeVellis, 2003, p. 103). Factor analyses were conducted to determine the basic components of the measure. "The factors provide a parsimonious account of reliable variance in the observed variables without significant loss of information" (Hoyle & Duvall, 2004, p. 301). This analysis also strengthens the measure's construct validity since there are not any external criteria available to measure the latent concept, community policing, (Champion, 2000).

As discussed earlier, there are two types of control variables used in this book: departmental and contextual. The departmental control variables were drawn from LEMAS 2003 data just like the community policing variables. Contextual control variables were drawn from Census 2000 data to control demographic variations across jurisdictions.

The first departmental control variable is "police size" (the number of police officers per 1,000 residents). According to Marvell and Moody (1996), an increase in number of police officers on the street can prevent crime through deterrence and incapacitation. Based on rational choice theory, criminals make their choices by calculating the costs and benefits of their actions. The criminals who observe more officers in the area are less likely to commit a crime due to the high risk of apprehension. The rise in the number of police officers might also increase the arrest rate and incapacitation, which, in turn, precludes offenders from committing more crimes (Tilley, 2006). Although studies yielded inconclusive results (Eck & Maguire, 2000; Levitt, 1997; Marvel & Moody, 1996; Sherman & Eck, 2006), controlling for police size is crucial for the accuracy of the study's findings. In order to create this variable, the number of all actual full-time and part-time sworn personnel who had general arrest powers was calculated. This sum was then divided by the population of the jurisdiction and multiplied by 1,000.

The second departmental control variable is the "percentage of community policing officers". Although the majority of police agencies in the U.S. shifted from traditional policing to community policing, it is difficult to claim that they all internalized the community policing philosophy throughout the entire department (Zhao et al., 2003). In some departments, community policing is implemented by only specialized units or personnel (Pelfrey, 2004). The implementation of community policing might solely be based on personnel specifically assigned to community policing activities. Therefore, it is important to control for the percentage of community policing officers within each department. To create this variable, all actual full-time sworn personnel with general arrest power were divided by the number of community policing officers and multiplied by 100.

The last departmental control variable is the "education requirement of officers" in the department. MacDonald (2002) argued that level of education can be used as a proxy for effective policing because the officers with a higher level of education are more likely to carry out effective crime control policies. In order to create this variable, the ordinal level original variable (minimum education requirement of new recruit officers ranging from 1 to 5) in the LEMAS 2003 survey was recoded as an indicator variable (0 = no college degree, and 1= some college degree).

Another important variable is the agency size. Similar studies (MacDonald, 2002; Beckman, 2006) overlooked small agencies which limited the generalizibility of their findings to only urban America (Weisheit, 2003). However, 78% of all the departments in the LEMAS 2003 survey are serving communities with a population fewer than 100,000. In addition, 69% of all the departments in the LEMAS 2003 survey are non-self-representative departments which employ fewer than 100 sworn police officers (BJS, 2006). These data suggest that MacDonald's (2002) and Beckman's (2006) inclusion strategy potentially disregarded two thirds of the sample departments in the LEMAS data.

In the literature, a number of studies examined various aspects of community policing across different size agencies and jurisdictions. The criterion used to classify an agency as *small* and *large* differs according to the researchers. For example, Zhao et al. (2002) used a population of 10,000 to categorize the agencies in two groups as small and large (small agency = population less than 10,000; large agency = population greater than 10,000). Zhao and Thurman (2003) used a population of 40,000 for the same purpose. The BJS (2006) and Beckman (2006) used the criterion of having 100 or more sworn officers in identifying the size of the agency. Oliver (2000), GAO (1995), Hawkins and Weisheit, (2003), Roth et al. (2004), Roth and Ryan (2000), and Wells and Weisheit (2004) all used a population of 50,000 to categorize agencies regarding their size (small agency = population less than 50,000; large agency = population greater than 50,000). In addition, the COPS office also used the criterion of population less than 50,000 when providing the Funding Accelerated for Smaller Towns (FAST) grants to the small agencies.

Consequently, in order to test the hypotheses of different effects regarding the size of the agency, the binary indicator variable "agency size" was created and used in this study. Agencies were categorized according to the population of the jurisdiction that they serve. Agencies serving a population equal to or fewer than 49,999 were identified as *small agencies* and coded as "0", while agencies serving a population equal to or greater than 50,000 were identified as *large agencies* and coded as "1".

Some structural factors such as poverty, racial diversity, populated neighborhood, and disrupted family structure are well-known correlates of crime (Lafree, 1998; Messner, 1982; Skolnick & Bayley, 1988; Sampson, 1987; Shaw & MacKay, 1942). These factors are important with regard to their effect on variation in crime rates across jurisdictions (Kornhauser, 1978; Palmiotto & Donahue, 1995); therefore, they must be controlled in any study examining crime rates across different places (Eck & Maguire, 2000).

Low economic status, ethnic heterogeneity, residential mobility, and family disruption are positively associated with crime and delinquency (Shaw & MacKay, 1942). In areas having such characteristics, social control is found to be weak, and the ability of the social structure to realize common values among its residents and to take care of its own problems is almost nonexistent (Kornhauser, 1978; Sampson, 1987; Sampson & Grove, 1989). Cities with higher percentages of divorced males, single-parent households, and unsupervised teenage peer groups have higher rates of crime and delinquency (Sampson, 1987; Sampson & Grove, 1989).

Such indicators of social disorganization are most prominent in African American, inner-city neighborhoods (Sampson & Wilson, 1995). Sampson (1987) argues that "racial differences in poverty and family disruption are so strong that the average contexts in which Whites reside are considerably better than the average context of Black communities" (p. 354). These low income neighborhoods that are situated in inner cities surrounded by business districts were not only occupied by Blacks, but also by individuals from a variety of different ethnic backgrounds. Since they do not share a common value system, and social networks in these communities are often deficient, they do not have meaningful bonds among neighbors which can also tie residents to the neighborhood itself (Reisig & Parks, 2004, p. 144). Typically, when these groups attain a certain level of wealth, they move to better places (Bursik & Grasmick, 1993). These more prosperous areas adhere to value systems which do not generally tolerate crime, disorder, and drug use (Sampson & Wilson, 1995).

MacDonald (2002) suggested that another important factor that affects crime rates is the number of motivated offenders (youths between the age 18 and 24). Even though a high percentage of youth in the population does not necessarily mean that all youths are potential offenders, there is substantial evidence available in the literature that age and crime are interrelated. The *age-crime curve* suggests that criminality follows the same track and peaks in the late teens and declines thereafter (Hirschi & Gottfredson, 1983).

The population, the percentage of urban population, the percentage of single female headed households with children under 17 years of age, the percentage of renters, the percentage of the population between the age of 18-24, the percentage of the population below poverty, the percentage of divorced males, and the percentage of African Americans were included in the study as jurisdiction-level structural variables. This enables the researcher to control for possible confounding factors of crime. These variables can be compiled from the Census 2000 data.

Models for Analysis

Three main models were used to test these hypotheses. Each model also had three sub-models. In the first model, the influence of predictor variables (community policing, departmental, and structural control variables) on each type of crime rate (property, violent, and total) were examined without separating agencies by their size. "Agency size" was included in the model as a departmental control variable. Each of three crime rates was separately used as the dependent variable, and thus, they respectively formed a sub-model. For example, property crime rate was regressed on all predictor variables, and it generated the first sub-model.

$$\hat{y}_{\text{(property, violent, total, crime per 1,000 residents)}} = a + b_1 x_1 + b_2 x_2 + b_3 x_3 + b_4 x_4 + b_5 x_5 + b_6 x_6 + b_7 x_7 + b_8 x_8 + b_9 x_9 + b_{10} x_{10} + b_{11} x_{11} + b_{12} x_{12} + e$$

The second main model only includes small agencies. Even though whether the effect of community policing practices depends on the agency size can be observed in the first model by examining interactions, the additional two models provide a clearer picture of the impact of community policing practices on crime rates separately for small and large agencies. Two additional main models also facilitate the interpretation of the study's findings regarding the second research question (*Is there a difference between small and large agencies in terms of the effect of community policing on crime rates?)* As stated above, each dependent variable was regressed on the predictor variables separately, and thus formed three sub-models.

$$\hat{y}_{\text{(property, violent, total, crime per 1,000 residents)}} = a + b_1 x_1 + b_2 x_2 + b_3 x_3 + b_4 x_4 + b_5 x_5 + b_6 x_6 + b_7 x_7 + b_8 x_8 + b_9 x_9 + b_{10} x_{10} + b_{11} x_{11} + e$$

The third main model only includes large agencies. The three sub-models were created and analyzed in the same way described above.

$$\hat{y}_{\text{(property, violent, total, crime per 1,000 residents)}} = a + b_1 x_1 + b_2 x_2 + b_3 x_3 + b_4 x_4 + b_5 x_5 + b_6 x_6 + b_7 x_7 + b_8 x_8 + b_9 x_9 + b_{10} x_{10} + b_{11} x_{11} + e$$

Where:

a = constant, X_1 = police size, X_2 = percentage of community policing officers, X_3 = education requirement for officers, X_4 = percentage of urban population, X_5 = percentage of single female headed household w/children under 17, X_6 = percentage of renters, X_7 = percentage of population between the age of 18-24, X_8 = the percentage of people living below the poverty level, X_9 = the percentage of divorced males, X_{10} = percentage of African Americans, X_{11} = community policing variables, X_{12} = agency size

Finally, the second and third main models were further analyzed in terms of the differences in effects. The z-test formula was used to examine differences in slopes between large and small agencies.

CHAPTER 5

The Impact of COP on Crime Rates

Initially, measures of level of implementation of community policing were generated. Then, these composite measures were further analyzed for their reliability and validity. Second, OLS regression analysis was conducted to determine whether there was an association between the level of implementation of community policing and crime rates. Finally, the researcher investigated whether this association (if any) differed based on the size of the agencies.

DATA SCREENING

Prior to factor and regression analyses, it is important to screen and clean the data. Frequency analyses indicated that 284 (10.6%) agencies had zero crime rates for the years 2004 and 2005. This finding illustrated that the data set had some errors.

Three main reasons were identified about why over 10% of agencies had zero crime rates. First, it was found that UCR data obtained through the Inter-University Consortium for Political and Social Research (ICPSR) differed from the UCR data available on the FBI website. For example, if an agency does not report crimes to the FBI for a specific year, this particular agency will not appear on the FBI's website even though this agency's actual number of crimes was entered as zero on the UCR data obtained through ICPSR. In short, it is not known whether these agencies' crime rates are really zero or just coded as zero.

Second, as explained earlier in the data merging process, agencies which responded to the LEMAS survey served as main subjects. These agencies were further merged with their associated UCR data. In some cases, agencies that participated in the LEMAS survey did not report crimes occurred in their jurisdictions to the FBI. For these agencies, the LEMAS and demographic variables are available in the merged data set, but their crime rates appear as zero since they simply did not report crimes to the FBI. In fact, these agencies' crime rates should have been coded as missing rather than zero.

Third, according to UCR data collecting procedure, if there are two different law enforcement agencies serving the same jurisdiction, offenses that occurred in this jurisdiction only appear for one agency. For example, if a sheriff's department and a police department serve together in the same jurisdiction, crime rates appear for only one department in order to preclude dual reporting. In addition, some sheriffs' departments basically do not deal with crime. These sheriff's departments administer jails and transport inmates. Therefore, they do not report any crime data to the FBI.

In order to verify the data set, the 284 agencies were doubled checked with the data available on the FBI web site to determine whether they actually had zero crime. Only two agencies, one in Minnesota and one in Pennsylvania, were identified as having actually reported zero crime to the FBI. Most of the zero crime data belong to the sheriff's departments. Additionally, 138 agencies which were listed as agencies having zero crime in the data set were identified as agencies in Illinois, the state from which the FBI received limited data for the years 2004 and 2005. It was observed that 282 agencies did not have any crime data. If they had been retained in the data set, they would have, at the very least, inflated the kurtosis score which, in turn, would have affected normality of dependent variables. The decision was made to include two agencies with actual zero crime rates, and to delete the 282 agencies. The analyses focused on the remaining 2,402 cases.

Normality, linearity, and homogeneity of variance for variables should also be tested. Since factor analysis and regression analyses were undertaken for different variables, data screening and assumption testing were discussed separately in the relevant section for each analysis.

GENERATING COMMUNITY POLICING VARIABLES

One of the problems in implementation and evaluation of community policing is the problem of the definition and the construct (Cheurprakobkit, 2002; Fielding, 2005). Many scholars defined community policing as a philosophy capturing a broad range of constructs rather than a program having a clear cut definition (Cordner, 1997; Greene & Mastrofski, 1988; Maguire & Katz, 2002; Trojanowicz & Bucqueroux, 1994; Wycoff, 1988). There are various conceptual definitions of community policing which create confusion regarding its meaning. Naturally, a lack of agreement on a single definition at the conceptual level precludes reaching a consensus on measurements of community policing. Acknowledging this problem, Colvin and Goh (2006) conducted a study to explore the underlying constructs of community policing and their validity. They used Cordner's (1997) four dimensions of community policing to explore the structure of the constructs. Colvin and Goh (2006) utilized an exploratory factor analysis that identified a six-factor model indicating an adequate fit to the data (p. 19). In addition to Cordner's four dimensions (philosophical, strategic, tactical, organization) their analyses yielded a need for two more dimensions: psycho-social and information.

In contrast to Colvin and Goh's (2006) study, the purpose of this book is neither to test a theory nor to create a new one about community policing. Using the community policing variables in the LEMAS 2003 data, the purpose of this book is to determine the level of implementation of community policing that is present in a law enforcement agency. It was hypothesized that agencies which implement community policing practices to a greater extent will have lower crime rates than agencies which implement community policing practices to a lesser extent. Thus, in terms of measurement, this book focuses on to what extent an agency implements community policing.

The variables in the "community policing" section of the LEMAS 2003 were utilized to measure the level of implementation of community policing in agencies. These variables and their coding are depicted in Table 1. All variables were dichotomous and coded as '0' and '1'.

Table 1

Community Policing Variables

No	Variable	Coding
1	New officer recruits received community policing training	0 = No 1 = Yes
2	In-service sworn personnel received community policing training	0 = No 1 = Yes
3	Civilian personnel received community policing training	0 = No 1 = Yes
4	Encouraged SARA type project	0 = No 1 = Yes
5	Conducted a citizen police academy	0 = No 1 = Yes
6	Maintained or created a formal, written community policing plan	0 = No 1 = Yes
7	Gave patrol officers responsibility for specific geographic areas/beats	0 = No 1 = Yes
8	Included collaborative problem-solving projects in the evaluation criteria of patrol officers	0 = No 1 = Yes
9	Trained citizens in community policing	0 = No 1 = Yes
10	Upgraded technology to support the analysis of community problems	0 = No 1 = Yes
11	Partnered with citizen groups and included their feedback in the development of neighborhood or community policing strategies	0 = No 1 = Yes
12	Mission statement includes community policing	0 = No 1 = Yes
13	Having a problem-solving partnership or written agreement with advocacy groups	0 = No 1 = Yes
14	Having a problem-solving partnership or written agreement with business groups	0 = No 1 = Yes
15	Having a problem-solving partnership or written agreement with faith-based organizations	0 = No 1 = Yes

Table 1

Community Policing Variables (Cond't)

16	Having a problem-solving partnership or written agreement with local government agencies	0 = No 1 = Yes
17	Having a problem-solving partnership or written agreement with other local law enforcement agencies	0 = No 1 = Yes
18	Having a problem-solving partnership or written agreement with neighborhood associations	0 = No 1 = Yes
19	Having a problem-solving partnership or written agreement with senior citizen groups	0 = No 1 = Yes
20	Having a problem-solving partnership or written agreement with school groups	0 = No 1 = Yes
21	Having a problem-solving partnership or written agreement with youth service organizations	0 = No 1 = Yes
22	Conducting or supporting a survey of citizens on public satisfaction with police services	0 = No 1 = Yes
23	Conducting or supporting a survey of citizens on public perception of crime/disorder problems	0 = No 1 = Yes
24	Conducting or supporting a survey of citizens on personal crime experiences of citizens	0 = No 1 = Yes
25	Conducting or supporting a survey of citizens on reporting of crimes to law enforcement by citizens	0 = No 1 = Yes
26	Conducting or supporting a survey of citizens on other topics	0 = No 1 = Yes

Table 1
Community Policing Variables(Cont.)

27	Using survey information for allocating resources targeted to neighborhoods	0 = No 1 = Yes
28	Using survey information for evaluating agency performance	0 = No 1 = Yes
29	Using survey information for evaluating officer performance	0 = No 1 = Yes
30	Using survey information for evaluating program effectiveness	0 = No 1 = Yes
31	Using survey information for prioritizing crime/disorder problems	0 = No 1 = Yes
32	Using survey information for providing information to patrol officers	0 = No 1 = Yes
33	Using survey information for redistricting beat/reporting areas	0 = No 1 = Yes
34	Using survey information for training development	0 = No 1 = Yes
35	Using survey information for other purposes	0 = No 1 = Yes

Using 35 separate dichotomous community policing variables in multivariate regression analysis, with each one being treated as an independent variable, is an impractical way to examine the relationship between community policing and crime rates. Since the first research question is interested in identifying the extent of community policing implementation in an agency, this approach is infeasible. Thus, two measurement strategies, creating a single *summated index* and conducting a *factor analysis* on these 35 variables, are more appropriate analyses. The former was created by summing the score for each item that corresponds to an agency. The latter technique determined which variables generated coherent subsets that were relatively independent of one another, and contained much of the information in the original 35 items (Tabachnick & Fidell, 2001; DeVellis, 2003). Instead of having a single variable, factor analysis might determine that there is more than one factor that can be used in multivariate regression analyses as explanatory variables. If there is more than one factor, this will be a manifestation of multidimensionality of the construct (community policing).

In addition, since the purpose is not testing or creating a theory about community policing, utilization of exploratory factor analysis (EFA) and confirmatory factor analysis (CFA) were not preferred (Nunnally & Bernstein, 1994).

COMMUNITY POLICING SUMMATED INDEX

A summated community policing index was generated by summing the score of each variable. The product of this summation provides a score for each agency indicating the agency's degree of involvement with community policing activities. The index score ranges from zero to 35. The lowest possible score that an agency can get on this index is zero, and the highest is 35.

Items and item-total correlations are depicted in Table 2. Item total correlations illustrate that only two items have a correlation below ".30". The correlation analysis suggests dropping these items from the index. The reliability score of the index is quite high (Cronbach $\propto$ = .926). It appears to be an acceptable level for research purposes. Once the two items having a correlation below .30 were dropped from the index, the alpha score reached .927. These two items were then retained because dropping them did not provide a drastic change in alpha score. The mean score for the index is 9.64 with a standard deviation of 7.84, and a skewness of .819.

Table 2

Item-Total Correlations for Community Policing Summated Index & Alpha

Item	Item-Total Correlation
New officer recruits received community policing training	.469
In-service sworn personnel received community policing training	.405
Civilian personnel received community policing training	.398
Encouraged SARA type project	.537
Conducted a citizen police academy	.475
Maintained or created a formal, written community policing plan	.517
Gave patrol officers responsibility for specific geographic areas/beats	.475
Included collaborative problem-solving projects in the evaluation criteria of patrol officers	.491
Trained citizens in community policing	.533
Upgraded technology to support the analysis of community problems	.464
Partnered with citizen groups and included their feedback in the development of neighborhood or community policing strategies	.580
Mission statement includes community policing	.444
Having a problem-solving partnership or written agreement with advocacy groups	.440
Having a problem-solving partnership or written agreement with business groups	.578
Having a problem-solving partnership or written agreement with faith-based organizations	.504
Having a problem-solving partnership or written agreement with local government agencies	.508
Having a problem-solving partnership or written agreement with other local law enforcement agencies	.409
Having a problem-solving partnership or written agreement with neighborhood associations	.593

Table 2

Item-Total Correlations for Community Policing Summated Index & Alpha (Cond't)

Having a problem-solving partnership or written agreement with senior citizen groups	.482
Having a problem-solving partnership or written agreement with school groups	.494
Having a problem-solving partnership or written agreement with youth service organizations	.524
Conducting or supporting a survey of citizens on public satisfaction with police services	.602
Conducting or supporting a survey of citizens on public perception of crime/disorder problems	.555
Conducting or supporting a survey of citizens on personal crime experiences of citizens	.606
Conducting or supporting a survey of citizens on reporting of crimes to law enforcement by citizens	.553
Conducting or supporting a survey of citizens on other topics	.183
Using survey information for allocating resources targeted to neighborhoods	.571
Using survey information for evaluating agency performance	.623
Using survey information for evaluating officer performance	.493
Using survey information for evaluating program effectiveness	.590
Using survey information for prioritizing crime/disorder problems	.575
Using survey information for providing information to patrol officers	.590
Using survey information for redistricting beat/reporting areas	.377
Using survey information for training development	.558
Using survey information for other purposes	.166
Cronbach Alpha: .926 n= 2,402	

FACTOR ANALYSIS

There are major differences between the *principal component analysis* and the factor analysis. Although they are interchangeably used, they differ both theoretically and mathematically (Cudeck, 2000).

Mathematically, in factor analysis, only shared variance is analyzed (Tabachnick & Fidell, 2001). The unique variance is excluded as it represents error (Nunnally & Bernstein, 1994). "Thus, the combinations we arrive at in extracting common factors are estimates of hypothetical error-free underlying variables" (DeVellis, 2003, p. 128). However, in principal component analysis both the common and unique variance of the variables are analyzed.

Theoretically, a factor is an underlying construct that causes the items to be answered as they are (DeVellis, 2003). The factor, in this case, is what causes a score on items. On the other hand, components are simply a reorganized version of the information in the actual item set. "They are merely aggregates of correlated variables. In that sense, the variables 'cause' or 'produce' the component" (Tabachnick & Fidell, 2001, p. 585).

In factor analysis, the purpose is to decide latent variables or dimensions which contribute to the pattern of correlations among the set of measured variables (Warner, 2008). In that sense, factor analysis is associated with theory development *(exploratory factor analysis* [EFA]), and theory testing *(confirmatory factor analysis* [CFA]) (Tabachnick & Fidell, 2001, p. 585). On the other hand, principal component analysis is generally used to reduce a set of items into a few components. Components are mathematically associated and do not necessarily reflect an underlying theory (Tabachnick & Fidell, 2001).

Consequently, principal component analysis was conducted to reduce 35 dichotomous variables to a few components. Components provide "parsimonious accounts of reliable variance in the observed variables without significant loss of information" (Hoyle & Duvall, 2004, p. 301). In fact, principal component analysis is not specifically designed for analyzing dichotomous variables. Kim and Mueller (1978) pointed out the problematic nature of factor analysis with dichotomous variables. However, they contended that dichotomous variables could be used if the correlations between variables are moderate (.7) or lower (pp. 74-75). Based on an inspection of the correlation matrix, it is observed that there is no correlation between variables greater than (.6). In spite of being dichotomous, these variables appear to be suitable for principal component analysis.

Assumptions in Principal Component Analysis

Principal component analysis operates under several assumptions: an adequate sample size, no outliers, no specification error, normality, homescedasticity, linearity, and the absence of multicollinearity. Some of these assumptions such as homescedasticity, multi-variate normality, and absence of multicollinearity are not critical for principal component analysis. In addition, since the variables are dichotomous, normality and linearity assumption are not strictly applied (Leech, Barrett, & Morgan, 2005). However, caution should be exercised with regard to outliers and the factorability of the data set.

Mertler and Vannatta (2005) suggested that with a categorical variable a split between 90-10 should be considered as an outlier variable and deleted. There were three variables which met this criterion. Initially, principal component analysis was undertaken by including these three variables. Next, these three items were excluded from the analysis. When these two results were compared, it was observed that the number of components remained the same along with the same items tapping the same components. Therefore, the outliers were retained for further analyses.

There are two main criteria in determining whether a particular data set is appropriate for factor analysis: the sample size and the strength of the relationship among the items (DeVellis, 2003). Although there is no specific rule to determine adequate sample size, Tabachnick and Fidell (2001) suggest that the number of cases should not be less than 300 in order to do factor analysis. In addition, DeVellis (2003) suggests that the rule of thumb for an adequate sample size is the larger the better in order to be able to generalize the results of factor analysis. However, Tinsley and Tinsley (1987) contend that the ratio of subjects to items is more important than the overall sample size. They suggest that a ratio of 5 to 10 subjects per item is acceptable. Since the sample size for this book was quite large (N = 2,402), the first criterion was met satisfactorily.

Nevertheless, additional caution should be demonstrated regarding the strength of the relationship because large sample sizes tend to produce smaller correlations (Tabachnick & Fidell, 2001). There are several tests to examine the strength of the relationship between variables such as Bartlett's test of sphericity (BTS), and the Kaiser, Meyer, Olkin (KMO) measure of sampling adequacy (Pallant, 2005).

The BTS is a test of the null hypothesis that the variables are unrelated. If the null hypothesis (the variables are unrelated) cannot be rejected, there is little reason to complete the factor analysis (Reinard, 2006). According to Tabachnick and Fidell (2001), "the KMO is a ratio of the sum of squared correlations to the sum of squared correlations plus the sum of squared partial correlations" (p. 589). Its index ranges from zero to one, and a minimum value of ".6" is desired for a good factor analysis.

The result of KMO and BTS tests and correlation matrix indicated that the strength of the relationship among the items was sufficient to conduct a factor analysis of the sample (KMO = .951; BTS = 43729.179, $p < .001$).

Extracting Components

Once the suitability of the data for factor analysis is justified, the next step is extracting factors (components). There are number of extraction techniques. In this book, principal component analysis, which is the most common and widely used technique, was utilized to extract the components (Tabachnick & Fidell, 2001). Principal component analysis extracts maximum variance from the variables out of a linear combination of observed variables to generate the first component. For the second component, residual correlations were used. That is, it removes the variance used for extracting the first component, and generates a second linear combination which explains the maximum proportion of the remaining variance (Garson, 2008). It is important to remember that principal component analysis generates the maximum number and nature of factors (Tabachnick & Fidell, 2001).

Like extraction techniques, there are several criteria to determine the number of components. The first one is Kaiser's criterion which is also known as the *eigenvalue rule*. It suggests dropping all components with an eigenvalue under 1. However, this rule has been criticized due to the possibility of overestimating the true number of components (Lance, Butts, & Michels, 2006). The results illustrated that five components had eigenvalues greater than 1 (Table 3). The most obvious break was between the first and second component. The second obvious break was between the second and the third component, but it was smaller than the first break.

Table 3
Principal Component Analysis of Community Policing Items

Component	Eigenvalue
1	10.52
2	4.00
3	1.88
4	1.14
5	1.09

The second criterion is Catell's scree test. It plots the components as the X axis and the corresponding eigenvalues as the Y axis (Garson, 2008). Catell's scree test suggests retaining the components above the point where the curve makes an elbow and becomes horizontal (Pallant, 2005). Like Kaiser's criterion, Catell's criterion has also been criticized. Sometimes the point where the elbow starts is not clear because the curve has multiple elbows or it is a smooth curve (Garson, 2008). Therefore, identifying the point is subject to the researcher's decision. Additionally, the number of components might be higher or lower than what the eigenvalue rule suggests. A visual inspection of the scree plot in Figure 5 illustrates that three components are above the elbow.

Due to the limitations of Kaiser's and Catell's tests, *parallel analysis,* which has recently started to gain popularity in the social sciences, is often recommended as a better technique to determine the number of components (Lautenschlager, 1988). "Parallel analysis involves comparing the size of the eigenvalues with those obtained from a randomly generated data set of the same size. Only those eigenvalues that exceed the corresponding values from the random data set are retained" (Pallant, 2005, p. 175). Using parallel analysis, only three components were retained (Table 4).

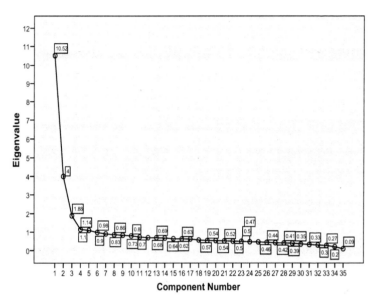

Figure 1. Community policing scree plot.

In addition to these three tests, a *reproduced correlation matrix* was utilized to validate the selection of three components. This matrix shows differences between the reproduced and actual correlations. If the residuals are large, the confidence in the selection of the number of components will be low (Warner, 2008). Based on an inspection of the reproduced correlation matrix, it was observed that there was no residual correlation with a value greater than .195. Since the percentage of non-redundant residual correlations with a value greater than .05 was only 18%, the selection of three components was supported. Consequently, three components were retained because, with the exception of Kaiser's criterion, all other criteria suggested three components.

Table 4

*Comparison of Principal Component Analysis Eigenvalues to Parallel
Analysis Criterion Values*

Component	Eigenvalue from PCA	Criterion Value from PA	Decision
1	10.52	1.23	Accept
2	4.00	1.20	Accept
3	1.88	1.18	Accept
4	1.14	1.16	Reject
5	1.09	1.14	Reject

Rotating Components

The next step in principal component analysis involves rotating
components to increase the interpretability of the solution. There are
numerous rotation techniques to choose. The major selection issue with
rotation techniques is to determine whether it is an *orthogonal* or
oblique rotation. In orthogonal rotation, the assumption is that
components are not correlated. Components might be interpreted more
easily with this technique, but its limitation is that it ignores the
possibility of a correlation among components. In oblique rotation, the
assumption is that components are correlated. This might be
disadvantageous in interpreting and reporting results; nevertheless, "it
does not arbitrarily impose the restriction that factors are uncorrelated"
(Kim & Mueller, 1978, p. 37), which might enable the researcher to
observe underlying conceptual process. The orthogonal rotation was
chosen because it is desirable to obtain dimensions that are independent
from each other, and reflect something that is not reflected by the other
dimensions.

SPSS offers three different orthogonal rotation techniques. There
are slight differences among these techniques. Tabachnick and Fidell
(2001) explained the differences:

> The goal of the varimax rotation is to maximize the
> variance of factor loadings by making high loadings
> higher and low ones lower for each factor,,, Quartimax
> does for variables what varimax does for factors...
> Equamax is a hybrid between varimax and quartimax

that tries simultaneously to simplify the factors and the
variables. (pp. 595-614)

These data were analyzed by utilizing all three orthogonal rotation
techniques that SPSS features. Each technique almost provided the
same component structure. Therefore, the most commonly used
varimax rotation solutions (variables and their factor loadings) are
depicted in Table 5.

Table 5
Factor Structure of Three-Component Model (Varimax Rotation)

Items	Components & Factor Loadings		
	1	2	3
Surveyed public satisfaction	**.812**	.217	.040
Surveyed public perception	**.807**	.199	.079
Surveyed personal crime experiences	**.749**	.162	.097
Surveyed reporting of crimes	**.756**	.123	.119
Used info for allocating resources	**.747**	.162	.125

.

Table 5
Factor Structure of Three-Component Model (Varimax Rotation) (Cond't)

Used info for evaluating agency performance	**.825**	.215	.065
Used info for evaluating officer performance	**.701**	.116	.073
Used info for evaluating program effectiveness	**.774**	.171	.120
Used info for prioritizing problems	**.766**	.122	.151
Used info for providing info to patrol officers	**.811**	.151	.101
Used info for redistricting areas	**.497**	.100	.100
Used info for training & development	**.715**	.189	.103
Encouraged SARA type projects	.180	**.603**	.211
Conducted citizen police academy	.204	**.511**	.168
Creating community policing plan	.203	**.508**	.252
Assigned officers to a specific geographic areas/beats	.114	**.519**	.228

Table 5
Factor Structure of Three-Component Model (Varimax Rotation)
(Cond't)

Problem-solving in officer evaluation criteria	.171	**.544**	.194
Training citizens in COP	.151	**.560**	.300
Upgraded technology	.129	**.526**	.217
Partnered with citizen groups	.167	**.567**	.341
Mission statement included COP	.127	**.534**	.149
Training new officers in COP	.089	**.687**	.073
Training (in service) sworn officers in COP	.052	**.643**	.044
Training civilian personnel in COP	.118	**.544**	.055
Partnership w/ advocacy groups	.098	.130	**.649**
Partnership w/ business group	.157	.284	**.677**
Partnership w/ religious groups	.149	.193	**.644**
Partnership w/ local government	.084	.213	**.689**
Partnership w/ other local law enforcement agencies	.087	.127	**.602**
Partnership w/ neighborhood associations	.154	.338	**.634**

Table 5

Factor Structure of Three-Component Model (Varimax Rotation) (Cond't)

Partnership w/ senior citizen groups	.148	.141	**.680**
Partnership w/ school groups	.093	.210	**.653**
Partnership w/ youth service organizations	.140	.188	**.699**
Surveyed other	.146	-.007	.114
Used info for other	.190	.057	.077
Percent Common Variance	30.062	11.426	5.385

The varimax rotated solution revealed a simple structure in which each component has a number of strong loadings. Except for two items (partnered with citizens group and partnership with other local law enforcement agency), all other items loaded on only one component.

Interpretation of Principal Component Analysis

Mathematical solutions based on principal component analysis revealed that community policing has three components. Before accepting and labeling these components, it is useful to note two limitations. First, it might be the case that the component structure solely reflects the survey structure. Second, it is possible that the community policing literature might not support the components, suggesting they might be mathematically formed.

Survey questions in the community policing section of LEMAS consist of five questions. The principal component analysis yielded that items from the last two questions (question 32a & 32b in the LEMAS survey) loaded on the first component which accounted for roughly 30% of the variation among items. Those items concern surveying the community on a number of topics, and the use of this information for various purposes. The second component accounted for roughly 11.5% of the variance among items. All items tapping into the second component were generated from responses given to the fourth question

(question 31 in the LEMAS survey). The items focus on having a problem-solving partnership or written agreement with various types of community groups. Consequently, the third component accounted for 5.3% of the variance among items. It was generated from the first three questions (question 28, 29, 30 in the LEMAS survey) in the community policing section of the LEMAS survey. Those questions concern training personnel and citizens in community policing, and activities regarding problem-solving.

Maguire and Mastrofski (2000) undertook exploratory factor analyses by using four different data sets to explore the dimensionality of community policing. They concluded that dimensions vary according to surveys and their items. They contended that the sponsoring agencies are somewhat coercive when grantees are preparing survey questions. Sponsoring agencies ask questions in a way that emphasizes what they determined are the necessary elements of community policing. That means the sponsoring agencies can ask somewhat leading questions, which, in turn, are very likely to influence the solution of exploratory factor analysis.

It is difficult to ascertain whether the LEMAS survey structure influences the component structure obtained in this study. Low explained variance (roughly 47%) suggests that there is a high level of error for which the principal component analysis solution cannot account. Nevertheless, it is difficult to identify what exactly causes this error.

It is important to have conceptual evidence to rule out the second concern which suggests components might just be mathematically formed. Since community policing does not have a clear conceptual and operational definition, it is difficult to label each scale in a way that everybody would agree. A number of scholars and practitioners have tried to define community policing conceptually by dividing it into dimensions, components, or objectives (Brown, 1989; Cordner, 1997; Eck & Maguire, 2000; Maguire, Kuhns, Uchida, & Cox, 1997; Manning, 1984; Roth & Ryan, 2000; Skolnick & Bayley, 1988). Others conducted research in order to determine the construct and dimensionality of community policing (Colvin & Goh, 2006; Fielding, 2005; Maguire & Mastrofski, 2000, Zhao, 1996). However, the literature still lacks consensus on a conceptual and operational definition of community policing. For that reason, components that emerged in this book might not exactly match other researchers' definitions.

Table 6

Cordner's Four Dimensions and Their Elements

Dimension	Element
Philosophical Dimension	
	Citizen input Broad function Personal service
Strategic Dimension	
	Reoriented operations Prevention emphasis Geographic focus
Tactical Dimension	
	Positive interaction Partnership Problem-solving
Organizational Dimension	
	Structure Management Information

Cordner's dimensions and elements of community policing (Table 6) and the four objectives of COPS and their associated items used by Roth et al. (2004) (Table 7) were used to provide evidence for the face and content validity of the scales. The purpose of the factor analysis utilized in this book is not to test Cordner's definition or COPS' objectives. However, cross matching the scales obtained through factor analyses with Cordner's and the COPS' definitions illustrate the scales' merit in providing measures for community policing (Table 9 & Table 11).

Table 7
COPS Four Objectives and Their Items

Objective	Item
Community Partnership	
	Joint crime prevention
	Regular community meetings
	Joint project with businesses
	Disorder reduction
	Citizen survey
	Clean up projects
	Citizens' board
	Citizen police academy
Problem-solving	
	Analyze problems with community
	Agency measure of response
	Systematic monitoring
	Community measures of response
	Residents identify problems
	Designate problems
	Analysts identify problems
	Consider neighborhood values
	Document problems/project
	Police/probation teams
Crime Prevention	
	School-based drug education
	Police/youth programs
	Non-auto patrol
	Late-night recreation
	Code enforcement confidential hotline
	Mediation
	Truancy prevention
	Victim assistance
	Battered women's programs
	Graffiti eradication programs

Table 7
COPS Four Objectives and Their Items (Cond't)

Organizational Change	
	Joint task force
	Alternative response methods
	Neighborhood patrol boundaries
	Beat integrity
	Mission/vision/values
	Team approach
	Community voice
	More officer discretion
	Multi-agency boundaries
	Revise employee evaluation

The First Component (Community Contribution)

According to the literature, community feedback is an important element in a community policing program (Vinzant & Crothers, 1994). Through information that flows from community to police, specific needs and opinions of the community can be obtained and appropriate responses can be generated. Moreover, collecting systematic information from the community strengthens the ability of police to prevent and control crime (Cordner, 1988; Eck & Sherman, 2006).

Table 8
Item-Total Correlations for Community Contribution Scale & Alpha

Items	Item-Total Correlation
Used info for evaluating agency performance	.829
Surveyed public satisfaction	.812
Used info for providing info to patrol officers	.787
Surveyed public perception	.796
Used info for evaluating program effectiveness	.753
Used info for prioritizing problems	.731
Surveyed reporting of crimes	.720
Surveyed personal crime experiences	.725

Table 8
Item-Total Correlations for Community Contribution Scale & Alpha (Cond't)

Used info for allocating resources	.717
Used info for evaluating officer performance	. 665
Used info for training & development	. 693
Used info for redistricting areas	.462
Cronbach alpha: .939 N = 2,402	

Utilizing the previously cited literature, the first scale relates to collecting systematic information from the public, and the use of that information for various departmental activities. Before labeling this scale, it was compared with Cordner's (1997) four dimensions and the COPS' four objectives in order to observe whether the content of this scale matches these two definitions (see Table 9 & Table 11).

Surveying the community on various topics obviously appeared in both definitions; however, placing it under a specific dimension seemed difficult. Surveys can be administered on numerous topics for various purposes. In conceptualizing Cordner's definition, this component is supposed to reflect two dimensions (see Table 9). The first part of the scale (collecting systematic information from the public) can be placed under the philosophical dimension (element = citizen input). The second part of the scale (use of that information for various departmental activities) can be placed under the organizational dimension (element = information). Although, Cordner (1997) contended that the first component should reflect two different dimensions, the principal component analysis of the LEMAS survey provided one component solution.

In terms of COPS' objectives, the first part (surveying citizens) matches with the item "citizen surveys" under the community partnership objective (see Table 11). The second part (the use of information for various types of departmental activity) might be placed under more than one objective such as organizational change (items = revise employee evaluation and neighborhood patrol boundaries) and problem-solving (item = residents identify problems).

Surveying the community and the use of information for specific purposes as stated in LEMAS are viewed as techniques for the community to contribute to policing. Hence, this component is labeled "community contribution". Agencies scoring on this component collected the community's ideas, perceptions, and experiences, and utilized this information for several departmental activities. In this way, the community contributed to how an agency policed the community. Even though labeling this component is subjective, available evidence (cross-matching with Cordner's dimensions and COPS' objectives) suggests that this component reflects a type of community policing activity.

Table 9

Cross-matching the Components with Cordner's Dimensions

Component No	Component	Dimension	Element
1	Community Contribution		
	Surveying citizens	Philosophical	Citizen Input
	Use of survey info	Organizational	Information
2	Training and Problem-solving		
	Mission statement	Organizational	Management
	Problem-solving & training	Tactical	Problem-solving
	Responsibility of beats	Strategic	Geographic focus
	Upgraded technology to analyze community problems	Organizational	Information
	Partnered with citizen groups and included their feedback in the development of neighborhood or community policing strategies	Philosophical	Citizen input Personal service
3	Problem solving Partnership	Tactical	Partnership Problem solving

The Second Component (Training and Problem-Solving)

Problem-solving activity has been the most prevalent community policing strategy in the last decade when compared to other strategies such as community partnership and organizational change (Roth et al., 2004). Most law enforcement agencies use the SARA model in problem-solving (Kappeler & Gaines, 2005). According to the growing body of research, problem-solving consistently shows a crime prevention effect. Therefore, it is expected that the increase in problem-solving efforts will result in less crime in the associated jurisdiction.

In addition, training and education are important parts of community policing programs. Without providing any training to personnel, any innovative policing program is likely to fail. The federal government funded many agencies to train their officers in community policing (Hickman et al., 2000). Both police personnel and the community should participate in community policing training and education in order to learn how to contribute to neighborhood's safety and how to collaboratively work with law enforcement agencies. Fridell and Wycoff (2004) suggest that citizen training in problem identification and resolution experienced the largest increase among other problem-solving techniques in police departments between 1992 and 2002. In the same way, Roth et al. (2004) contended that between 1998 and 2000 the most common crime prevention programs were education programs.

A few other items loaded on this component such as upgraded technology and a mission statement that included community policing. Attempts to match this component with the Cordner and COPS definitions are somewhat more problematic because items match with all four objectives of COPS, and with all Cordner's four dimensions. Because a greater number of items was related to two areas (training and problem-solving), this component was labeled as "training and problem-solving".

Table 10
Item-Total Correlation for Training & Problem-solving Scale & Alpha

Items	Coding
Training new officers	.550
Training sworn officers	.483
Encouraged SARA type projects	.575
Training civilians	.431
Mission statement included COP	.471
Problem-solving in officer evaluation criteria	.518
Assigned geographic areas/beats	.492
Trained citizens in COP	.569
Partnered with citizen groups	.589
Upgraded technology	.495
Conducted citizen police academy	.486
Creating community policing plan	.519
Cronbach alpha: .847 N = 2,402	

Third Component (Problem-solving Partnership)

Problem-solving represents the idea of shifting from incident-based reactive policing to the problem-oriented proactive policing (Goldsein, 1990). Police departments by themselves are not able to identify and solve community specific problems. Both in identifying problems and in generating responses, the community is a key element (Pate & Shtull, 1994). Law enforcement agencies should collaborate with the community, other agencies, and different neighborhood entities in order to address significant problems and share responsibility with community (Cordner, 1997).

Table 11
Cross-matching the Components with COPS' Objectives

Comp. No	Component & Main Items	Objective	Element
1	Community Contribution		
	Surveying citizens	Community Partnership	Citizen Survey
	Use of survey info	Organizational Change	Revised Employee Evaluation
		Problem-solving	Resident identify problem
2	Training and Problem-Solving		
	Mission statement	Organizational Change	Mission/vision/values
	Problem-solving & training	Community Partnership	Citizen police academy
		Crime Prevention	School based drug education
	Responsibility of beats	Organizational Change	Geographic focus

Table 11
Cross-matching the Components with COPS' Objectives (Cond't)

	Upgraded technology to analyze community problems	Problem-solving	Systematic monitoring (GIS)
	Partnered with citizen groups and included their feedback in the development of neighborhood or community policing strategies	Organizational Change	Community Voice
3	Problem-Solving Partnership		
		Community Partnership Problem-solving	Joint crime prevention Regular meetings Joint project w/ businesses Analyzing problem w/ community

In the same way, quality of life issues can be improved by working collaboratively with community organizations, businesses, and other agencies. When community members actively engage in problem-solving strategies, a sense of community and community cohesion are increased which, in turn, might inhibit illegal activities in the neighborhood (Bayley, 1996; Sampson & Grove, 1989). Various activities might be classified under the umbrella of community partnership. Active participation of community members and organizations in crime prevention strategies such as neighborhood watch might be a good example of a community partnership. In addition, cooperation between law enforcement agencies and various community groups such as working with the municipality to remove graffiti from the neighborhood can also be considered community partnership. In either situation, the community and the police are viewed as co-producers of public safety (Greene, 2000).

Table 12
Item-Total Correlations for Problem-solving Partnership Scale & Alpha

Items	Item-Total Correlation
Partnership w/ youth service organizations	.646
Partnership w/ senior citizen groups	.607
Partnership w/ local government	.639
Partnership w/ advocacy groups	.564
Partnership w/ school groups	.604
Partnership w/ business group	.664
Partnership w/ religious group	.593
Partnership w/ other local law enforcement agency	.525
Partnership w/ neighborhood associations	.636
Cronbach alpha: .871 n = 2,402	

In terms of Cordner's dimensions, the problem-solving partnership component can be placed under the tactical dimension. Two elements (partnership and problem-solving) perfectly match with this component. In terms of COPS' four objectives, this component might be placed both under the community partnership and the problem-solving objectives. There is a possibility of ambiguity in this case. Two elements (problem-solving and partnership) in Cordner's dimensions fit under the tactical dimension; whereas, the same two elements represent two separate objectives in the COPS' definition.

Consequently, items in the LEMAS survey refer to a problem-solving partnership or written agreement with several different community entities. Therefore, this component is labeled as "problem-solving partnership".

RELIABILITY AND VALIDITY OF SCALES

DeVellis (2003) and Warner (2008) contend that there are eight steps in scale development. Since this book is utilizing secondary data, primary steps such as creating a pool of items and administering items to a sample were already completed. Therefore, the first step in scale development for this study is conducting principal component analysis to assess the number and nature of components. Next, an additive scale was generated for each of three components based on the principal component analysis solutions. Each item's score within a component was summed. Thus, the product of each component generated a continuous variable which can be used in OLS regression analysis in compliance with its assumptions. The last step is assessing the scale's reliability and validity.

Warner (2008) contends that Cronbach alpha tells us "how reliable our estimate of the 'stable' entity" that is measured is (p. 854). Cronbach alpha can be used even with dichotomous variables to illustrate internal consistency among variables. A large alpha value indicates all items in a scale measure the same latent variable (DeVellis, 2003).

The community contribution scale consists of 12 dichotomous items. The scale scores range from zero to 12. The alpha of this scale is .939 with a mean of 1.98, and a standard deviation of 3.41. The problem-solving partnership scale consists of nine items. The scale scores range from zero to nine. The alpha of this scale is .868 with a mean of 2.95, and a standard deviation of 2.88. The training and problem-solving scale consists of 12 items. The scale scores range from zero to 12. The alpha of this scale is .852 with a mean of 4.70, and a standard deviation of 3.45. All three of the scales' alpha values are high reaching the acceptable level for research purposes. Limited by the use of secondary data, it can be claimed that these three scales are reliable measures of the constructs that they are deemed to represent.

DeVellis (2003) contended that "...determining that a scale is reliable does not guarantee the latent variable shared by the items is, in fact, the variable of interest to the researcher" (p. 49). Hence, the validity of the scales should also be ensured. There are several types of measurement validity such as content, face, criterion, and construct. For researchers, it is not always possible to illustrate all types of validity for their measurement. In particular, for community policing, establishing validity which requires existing tests (convergent validity) or existing measures (criterion-oriented validity) is problematic. As previously discussed, community policing lacks a single concrete underlying theory and agreed upon constructs even though scholars have attempted to create one (Colvin & Goh, 2006; Cheurprakobkit,

2002; Fielding, 2005; Maguire, Kuhns, Uchida, & Cox, 1997; Maguire & Mastrofski, 2000, Zhao, 1996).

Both face and content validity are related to the content of the items (Warner, 2008). When a subset of the items from a universe is randomly established, in theory, a scale has content validity (DeVellis, 2003). Content validity has two major standards: a representative collection of items, and sensible methods of test construction. Establishing content validity is often infeasible for community policing due to the fact that neither the domain (community policing) nor the sampling unit is well defined (Nunnally & Bernstein, 1994, p. 102).

Another option is to use experts to inspect the items' relevance to the content. Although specific experts were not asked to inspect the items in the survey, the items were attempted to be cross matched with items in the experts' published definitions. Cordner's definition which includes a broad range of elements within the context of community policing was used to validate the items in the survey. Second, items that were used by Roth et al. (2004) to explore trends in agencies' implementation of community policing according to COPS' four major objectives were used for the same purpose.

As a result, it is observed that the items in the three scales are included in both Cordner's and the COPS's lists. Nevertheless, matching the components that the principal component analysis solution provided with Cordner's dimensions and COPS' objective was problematic. Similarly, earlier studies that attempted to validate Cordner's dimensions also resulted in different pattern constructs (Colvin & Goh, 2006; Cheurprakobkit, 2002).

Face validity of a measurement refers to whether the measurement appears to measure what it intends to measure (Warner, 2008). DeVellis (2003) suggested that a definition like this is problematic for several reasons. For example, "it is unclear to whom an instrument's purpose should be evident, on its face. Is it the respondent? ...Is it the person creating the instrument who should recognize the purpose" (p. 58)? In terms of face value, LEMAS labeled the section "community policing". Thus, the researchers obviously defined the variables as community policing variables. Nevertheless, it is difficult to claim that the respondents agree with the researcher's definition of community policing without any additional information.

The validity of a summated community policing index seems less problematic than the validity of the scales. With a single summated index, the underlying construct that is deemed to be measured is the level of implementation of community policing in an agency. Even though the items do not encompass the whole spectrum of the content of community policing, it is argued that they represent some part of community policing activities out of the whole universe of community policing activities. In fact, it is almost impossible to list the full range of items that reflects an abstract theory or philosophy like community policing.

Face validity was not guaranteed for each scale. It is hard to determine the linkage between the scale and a specific construct. For example, it is problematic whether surveying citizens and the use of survey information (first scale) represent an organizational change, partnership with community, problem-solving, or a combination of all three. However, according to the available literature, it appears that each scale measures an aspect of community policing. Determining which aspect is measured by a scale varies according to which specific definition of community policing the researcher utilized.

It is not surprising to identify measures (scales) whose validity is questionable if the intent is to measure the presence of community policing. Maguire and Mastrofski (2000) contended that since community policing does not have dominant theories or definitions behind it, using exploratory or confirmatory methods are likely to cloud the picture rather than clarify it (p. 34). At this point, Bayley's (1998b) and Moore's (1994) criticisms that true evaluation of community policing is nearly impossible can be applied to the study.

Limited with the traditional validity concerns in community policing studies, three scales were used rather than a summated index. The use of three scales enabled the researcher to separately explore the direction of the relationship between each dimension of community policing and crime rates. It also provides the relative importance of one dimension over the others. Therefore, despite the validity concern, three scales are thought to be a better choice.

DESCRIPTIVE STATISTICS

The subjects of this study consist of 881 (36.7%) large and 1,521 (63.3%) small law enforcement agencies. Table 13 shows the general characteristics of the sample. On average, there are 2.16 officers per 1,000 residents. Approximately, 1,949 (81.1%) of the agencies do not require a college degree or any college credits for new police officer hires. Only 403 (18.9%) agencies require college credits or a college degree for new recruits. On average, 12.65% of the officers are community policing officers.

Table 13
Descriptive Statistics for All Variables

Variable	Mean	SD	Min	Max
Departmental Control Variables				
Police Size[2]	2.16	1.77	.11	24.46
COP Officers[3]	12.65	27.79	0	100
Education Requirement[4]	.19	.39	0	1
Agency Size[4]	.37	.48	0	1
Structural Control Variables				
Population[5]	108,231.51	356,695.76	67	9,519,378
Urbanized Area[3]	75.76	34.94	0	100
Single female households [3]	7.09	3.20	0	25.30
Renters[3]	30.35	12.69	1.22	81.43
Population 18-24 years of age[3]	9.53	5.00	1.15	67.78
Population below poverty[3]	12.82	7.42	0	51.93
Divorced Males[3]	4.33	1.29	0	14.70
African American Population[3]	10.96	15.99	0	95.67
Explanatory Variables				
Community Contribution[1]	1.98	3.41	0	12
Problem-Solving Partnership[1]	3.03	2.91	0	9
Training & Problem-Solving[1]	4.87	3.44	0	12
COP Summated Index[1]	9.94	7.89	0	35
Dependent Variables				
Property Crime Rate[2]	29.82	25.82	0	243.09
Violent Crime Rate[2]	12.56	12.73	0	166.13
Total Crime Rate[2]	42.38	37.48	0	349.39

Note: n = 2,402

In 758 (31.6 %) agencies there is no community policing officer; whereas, in 61 (2.5 %) agencies all personnel are community policing officers. In 166 (6.9%) agencies, there is no identifiable community policing activity.

In terms of community policing variables, agencies' average score on the community contribution scale is 1.93 with a standard deviation of 3.31. On average, agencies score 3.03 with a standard deviation of 2.95 on the problem-solving partnership scale. The highest mean score (4.87) is on the training and problem-solving scale with a standard deviation of 3.44. These statistics illustrate that, on average, the level of implementation of community policing is low.

Each agency's jurisdiction has unique characteristics. Demographics of each jurisdiction are likely to influence crime rates. The average population of the sample is 108,231 with a standard deviation of 356,695. For example, the Loving County Sheriff Office has the smallest population (67), and Los Angeles County Sheriff's Office has the largest population (9,519,378). On average, 75% of the jurisdictions are urbanized areas, roughly 7% of the sample is a single female headed household with children under 17 years of age, and almost 30% of the sample is renting a home or an apartment. The mean percent of youth who are between 18 and 24 years old age is 9.53 with a standard deviation of 5.00. On average, 12.82% of the sample lives in poverty, and 4.33% of men are divorced. The mean percent of African Americans is 10.96 with a standard deviation of 15.99.

The number of property crimes per 1,000 resident ranges from zero to roughly 243 with a mean of 29.82 and a standard deviation of 25.82. The average number of violent crimes per 1,000 residents is 12.56 with a standard deviation of 12.73. On average, there are 42.38 total crimes per 1,000 residents with a standard deviation of 37.48.

BIVARIATE CORRELATIONS

Bivariate correlations were undertaken to assess the strength of the relationships among variables and to determine the multi-collinearity. The correlation matrix is presented in Table 14.

As expected, all demographic control variables are positively associated with each type of crime rate. Specifically, the percentage of urbanized area, the percentage of single female headed households with children under 17 years of age, the percentage of renters, the percentage of the population between 18 and 24 years of age, the percentage of population living below poverty level, the percentage of divorced men, and the percentage of African Americans are all positively associated with property, violent, and total crime rates. This provides some support for the social disorganization theory and the related literature. The highest correlation is between the violent crime rate (the number of violent crimes per 1,000) and the percentage of single female headed households with children under 17 years of age (r = .495 p < .01). The next highest positive correlations are between crime rates and the percentage of renters in the associated jurisdiction. They are all moderate correlations and slightly above .40 (p < .01). Correlations between crime rates and departmental control variables are also in the expected direction, with the exception of the percentage of community policing officers. Police size (the number of officer per 1,000 residents) is positively associated with crime rates, but the correlations are all weak and are slightly over .10 (p < .01).

Table 14

Bivariate Correlations among Variables

	1	2	3	4	5	6	7	8	9	10	11	12	13	14	15	16	17
1 Police Size	-																
2 COP Officers	.195**	-															
3 Education Requirement	-.068**	-.002	-														
4 Agency Size	-.255**	-.192**	.081**	-													
5 Urbanized Population	-.005	-.175**	.148**	.291**	-												
6 Single female households	.115**	-.051*	-.096**	.104**	.190**	-											
7 Renters	.122**	-.065**	-.057**	.223**	.363**	.555**	-										
8 Population b/w 13-24 years of age	-.055*	-.078**	.016	.151**	.206**	.193**	.481**	-									
9 Population below poverty	.070**	.014	-.181**	-.008	-.110**	.652**	.549**	.408***	-								
10 Divorced Males	.061**	.036	-.104**	-.001	-.158**	.185**	.146**	-.123**	.180**	-							
11 African American	.0146*	-.060**	-.103**	.116**	.125**	.713**	.353***	.154***	.470**	.019	-						
12 Community Contribution	-.015	-.008	.103**	.209**	.193**	.033	.125***	.077**	-.024	-.005	.047***	-					
13 Problem Solving Partnership	-.054*	-.034	.133**	.351**	.276**	.075**	.214**	.115*	-.002	-.021	.067***	.345***	-				

Table 14
Bivariate Correlations among Variables (Cond't)

	1	2	3	4	5	6	7	8	9	10	11	12	13	14	15	16	17
14 Training & Problem Solving	-.023	-.005	.148**	.403**	.409**	.086**	.267**	.144**	-.046*	-.018	.085*	.450**	.585**	-			
15 Property Crime Rate	.410**	-.005	.026	.049**	.356**	.361**	.418**	.154**	.240**	.190*	.275**	.174**	.176**	.310**	-		
16 Violent Crime rate	.309**	-.004	-.030	.052**	.284**	.495**	.419**	.159**	.354**	.218**	.389**	.113**	.145**	.259**	.764**	-	
17 Total Crime Rate	.398**	-.005	.008	.053**	.351**	.428**	.442**	.165**	.293**	.211**	.330**	.163**	.175**	.310**	.974**	.890**	**

Note: ** Pearson Correlation Coefficients p < .01 (2–tailed)
* Pearson Correlation Coefficients p < .05 (2–tailed) n = 2,401

Agencies having a greater number of police officers per 1,000 residents are more likely to have higher crime rates. This finding is consistent with the literature that indicates that an increase in the number of officers is not associated with a reduction in crime rates (Marvel & Moody, 1996; Eck & Maguire, 2000). The percentage of community policing officers and education requirements for new recruits are significantly associated with crime rates. Agency size has positive weak correlations with each type of crime rate (around .050; p < .01). These findings suggest that larger agencies are more likely to have higher crime rates.

The first three hypotheses indicate that an increase in the level of implementation of community policing is negatively associated with crime rates. In contrast to these hypotheses, it is observed that each scale measuring the level of implementation of one dimension of community policing is positively associated with all crime rates. That is, once any type of implementation of community policing increases, crime rates also increase. Community contribution has weak positive associations with crime rates. The highest correlation is with the property crime rate (r = .174; p < .01), and the lowest correlation is with violent crime rate (r = .113; p < .01). Agencies which administered or sponsored a citizen survey, and used the survey information for various departmental activities are more likely to have higher rates for each type of crime. Additionally, problem-solving partnership also has weak positive correlations with crime rates. Agencies which have a written agreement or problem-solving partnership with any community entity are more likely to have higher rates for each type of crime. The highest correlation is with the property crime rate (r = .176, p < .01), and the lowest correlation is with the violent crime rate (r = .145, p < .01). The training and problem-solving variable has a moderate correlation with each type of crime rate. Both property and total crime rates moderately correlate with training and problem-solving (r = .310, p < .01). Agencies which trained their personnel and citizens, using SARA type projects and various types of community policing activities, are more likely to have higher rates of crime.

The highest correlations occur among the dependent variables. This is not surprising because all dependent variables measure crime. These high correlations do not pose a threat to the OLS regression assumptions since each type of crime rate would be used as a dependent variable for a separate regression model. In general, multi-collinearity is not a problem except for two strong positive correlations. The percentage of single female headed households with children under 17 years of age is highly correlated with both the percentage of African Americans ($r = .713$, $p < .01$), and the percentage of the population living below poverty level ($r = .652$, $p < .01$). In regression analyses, tolerance and variation inflation factor (VIF) scores will be examined in order to ensure that these variables do not violate the multi-collinearity assumption. High correlations between these variables are consistent with the literature which indicates African American communities are devastated by poverty and disrupted families. Single female headed households are more prevalent in these communities where men often serve time in correctional institutions, are murdered, or divorced (Cole, 1999).

OLS REGRESSION ANALYSES

Assumption Testing

In order to test the hypotheses, OLS regression analyses were performed. The assumptions of the OLS regression were also tested. Testing the regression assumptions is important because significance levels, confidence intervals, and other tests are sensitive to a violation of these assumptions (Norusis, 2000). It is very rare in the social sciences for a study to satisfy all of the regression assumptions perfectly; however, caution should be exercised in determining to what extent a possible violation influences the regression results. Assumptions of linearity, homescedasticity, normality, outliers, auto correlation, and multi-collinearity were investigated for each regression model.

To detect multivariate outliers, first, Mahalanobis' distance was examined. Mahalanobis' distance is a measure of how much a case's values on the independent variables differ from the average of all cases. It can be assessed for each case by using $\chi 2$ distribution. The examination of Mahalanobis' distances revealed that for each regression model there were several multivariate outlier cases. These cases had extreme values on more than one variable. Since the number of outliers accounted for no more than 4% of all cases, they were not automatically excluded. Nevertheless, Mertler and Vannatta (2005) contended that if a case or a set of cases is extreme enough, it can make a regression coefficient significant when, in fact, it is not significant without these extreme cases.

The researcher exercised caution to determine to what extent these outliers might influence regression results. Cook's distance is a test to measure the change in all regression coefficients when a case is deleted from the model (Norusis, 2000). A large Cook's distance value indicates that deleting a specific case will substantially change the regression coefficients. Norusis (2000) and Tabachnick and Fidell (2001) suggested that a Cook's value greater than 1 needs to be investigated further. Each regression model was also checked with a Cook's distance test. None of the regression models had a Cook's value reaching 1. Therefore, no outlier case was excluded from the analyses.

The assumptions of linearity, normality, and homescedasticity were tested for each regression model. Norusis (2000) contended that studentized residuals are superior over standardized residuals in identifying possible violations of regression assumptions. While studentized residuals take into account the differences in variability for each point, the observed residuals are divided by the same number to compute standardized residuals. Both standardized and studentized residuals were examined for violations of assumptions.

In the case of a moderate violation of these assumptions, the immediate remedy is to transform variables (Tabachnick & Fidell, 2001; Mertler & Vannatta, 2005; Norusis, 2000). For positively skewed variables, natural log and square root transformations were performed. For one negatively skewed variable, reflect log and square root transformations were undertaken. Several regression models were run both with transformed and original variables for each regression model. Since no substantial improvement was observed in satisfying regression assumptions with the transformed variables, original variables were utilized for regression analyses. The severe multi-collinearity assumption was also tested. Multi-collinearity refers to a high correlation among two or more predictor variables. For a violation of this assumption, standard errors of the variables are inflated which, in turn, influence the significance of the regression coefficients. VIF and Tolerance statistics were used to test this assumption. The tolerance statistic is computed by one minus squared multiple correlations and the VIF statistic is computed by 1/ tolerance score. A tolerance value lower than .25, and a VIF value higher than 4 are an indication of multi-collinearity (Pallant, 2005). Although tolerance and

VIF values were not threatening, two highly correlated variables based on bivariate correlation results were further tested for multi-collinearity (the percentage of single female households with children under 17 years of age highly correlates with the percentage of African Americans $r = .713$, $p < .01$). Regression analyses were performed both including and excluding one of these variables. The significance of the regression coefficients was not drastically changed for interpretation purposes, thus both of them were included in the analyses reported.

The first three hypotheses were tested in all models. By separately utilizing property, violent, and total crime rates, the hypothesis (if the level of implementation of community policing increases, the crime rates will decrease) was tested. In split and comparison models, the second three hypotheses (there is a difference between large and small agencies in terms of the effect of level of implementation of community policing on crime rates) were tested by separately regressing property, violent, and total crime rates on predictor variables. For each model, findings were reported for departmental control variables, contextual control variables, and community policing variables, respectively.

Regression Model for Property Crime Rates

In this section, the first hypothesis is tested. It stated that if the level of implementation of community policing increases, the property crime rates will decrease. Even though no hypothesis is established for predictor variables other than those related to community policing, the findings regarding those control variables are also discussed.

In terms of departmental control variables, the variables "police size" and "education requirements" have a positive impact on property crime rates. Agencies that require college credits or a college degree for new recruits and employ more officers are more likely to have higher property crime rates. Agency size has a negative impact on the dependent variable. This finding suggests that larger agencies are likely to have lower property crime than smaller agencies. More specifically, larger agencies have roughly three fewer property crimes per 1,000 residents than small agencies ($b = -3.068$, $p < .01$).

The model illustrates that except for the variables "African Americans" and "population between 18 and 24 years of age", all other structural level variables have a significant positive effect on property crime rates. That is, jurisdictions having more divorced males, more

Table 15

Regression of Property Crime Rates on Predictor Variables

Variable	Coefficient	Beta	t
Police Size[2]	5.301***	.364	21.816
COP Officers[3]	-.025	-.024	.-1.501
Education[4] Requirement	2.590*	.039	2.466
Agency Size[4]	-3.068**	-.057	-3.144
Urbanized Area[3]	.197***	.266	13.241
Single Female Households[3]	.652**	.081	2.861
Renters[3]	.188***	.093	3.903
18-24 Years of Age[3]	.050	.010	.503
Below Poverty[3]	.365***	.009	4.104
Divorced Males[3]	3.432***	.171	10.295
African American[3]	.058	.036	1.605
Community Contribution[1]	.229	.029	1.697
Training & Problem-Solving[1]	1.435***	.192	8.866
Problem-Solving Partnership[1]	-.099	-.011	-.581
Constant	-33.745***		-17.912
R^2 = .442 F = 134.827 S_e = 19.35031 n = 2,402			

Note: *** $p < .001$, ** $p < .01$, * $p < .05$

people living below poverty level, more renters, more single female headed households with children under 17 years of age, and are in more urbanized areas are more likely to have higher property crime rates.

Only the training and problem-solving dimension of community policing activity reached statistical significance. In contrast to the hypothesis, it has a positive impact on property crime rates. Agencies that implement more activities related to the training and problem-solving dimension of community policing are more likely to have higher property crime rates.

The variables "police size", "urbanized area", "training and problem-solving" and "divorced males" respectively make the strongest unique contribution to predicting property crime rates when other variables in the model are controlled. The model itself explained roughly 44% of the variance in property crime rates.

Regression Model for Violent Crime Rates

In this section, the second hypothesis which states that an increase in the level of implementation of community policing is likely to result in a decline in violent crime rates is tested. Results depicted in Table 16 illustrate that, in contrast to the previous model, the education requirement is not a significant predictor. Agencies with a greater number of police officers per 1,000 residents have higher violent crime rates. In addition, agency size negatively affects the violent crime rates; i.e., larger agencies have lower violent crime rates. As in the previous model, the percentage of community policing officers is not a significant factor.

In terms of structural level variables, the analysis reveals that urbanized areas, single female headed households with children under 17 years of age, divorced males, African Americans, and people living below the poverty level all have significant positive effects on violent crime rates. The two variables, "African Americans" and "renters" never reached statistical significance.

As in the previous model, only the training and problem-solving dimension of community policing has a positive significant impact on violent crime rates. Contrary to the study's hypothesis, agencies that train citizens and personnel, and use various problem-solving techniques are more likely to have higher violent crime rates. The other two dimensions of community policing did not approach statistical

Table 16

Regression of Violent Crime Rates on Predictor Variables

Variable	Coefficient	Beta	t
Police Size[2]	1.735***	.242	14.162
COP Officers[3]	-.004	-.008	-.420
Education[4] Requirement	.297	.009	.561
Agency Size[4]	-1.500**	-.057	-3.049
Urbanized Area[3]	.075***	.206	10.019
Single Female Households[3]	.896***	.225	7.796
Renters[3]	.020	.020	.821
18-24 Years of Age[3]	.029	.012	.588
Below Poverty[0]	.236***	.138	5.258
Divorced Males[3]	1.690***	.171	10.056
African American[3]	.066***	.082	3.576
Community Contribution[1]	-.044	-.012	-.653
Training & Problem-Solving[1]	.703***	.190	8.611
Problem-Solving Partnership[1]	-.053	-.012	-.620
Constant	-17.823***		-17.294
R^2 = .416 F = 121.444 S_e = 9.75629 n = 2,402			

Note: *** $p < .001$, ** $p < .01$, * $p < .05$

significance. Overall, this model explains 42% of the variance in violent crime rates. The strongest unique contributors are "police size", "single female headed households with children under 17", "training and problem-solving", and "urbanized area" respectively.

Regression Model for Total Crime Rates

In this section, the third hypothesis, if the level of implementation of community policing increases, total crime rates will decrease, was tested. Similar to the property crime rates model, "education requirement" and "police size" are significant predictors of the model. Agencies having more police officers and those that require college credits or a college degree for new recruits are more likely to have higher total crime rates. Total crime rates are also more likely to be higher for smaller agencies serving a population below 50,000 than for larger agencies serving a population over 50,000.   Except   for   the percentage of youth in the population (youth 18-24 years of age), all structural level variables (the percentage of urbanized area, single female households with children under 17 years of age, renters, people living below poverty, divorced males, African Americans) have significant positive effects on total crime rates. Where these percentages increase, the total crime rates also increase.

Consistent with two previous models, the training and problem-solving dimension of community policing has a positive significant impact on total crime rates. The other two dimensions of community policing were never close to statistical significance. The predictors altogether account for roughly 47% of the variance in total crime rates. The four strongest unique contributors are "police size", "urbanized area", "training and problem-solving", and "divorced males", respectively.

Summary of Findings for Full Models

For each of the full models, the percentage of community policing officers, the percentage of people between 18 and 24 years of age, the community contribution and the problem-solving partnership dimensions of community policing never reached statistical significance.

Table 17

Regression of Total Crime Rates on Predictor Variables

Variable	Coefficient	Beta	t
Police Size[2]	7.036***	.342	21.063
COP Officers[3]	-.029	-.020	-1.246
Education[4] Requirement	2.888*	.031	1.999
Agency Size[4]	-4.568**	-.060	-3.405
Urbanized Area[3]	.272***	.260	13.306
Single Female Households[3]	1.548***	.136	4.940
Renters[3]	.208**	.072	3.141
18-24 Years of Age[3]	.079	.011	.561
Below Poverty[3]	.601***	.122	4.913
Divorced Males[3]	5.123***	.181	11.176
African American[3]	.124*	.054	2.479
Community Contribution[1]	.184	.017	.995
Training & Problem-Solving[1]	.703***	.190	8.611
Problem-Solving Partnership[1]	-.152	-.012	-.650
Constant	-51.568***		-18.350
$R^2 = .471$ F = 152.052 $S_e = 26.602726$ n = 2,402			

Note: *** $p < .001$, ** $p < .01$, * $p < .05$

Agencies accepting recruits having a college degree or some college credits are more likely to have higher property and total crime rates. However, this finding is not significant for violent crime rates. Interestingly, the only negative relationship detected between agency size and crime rates suggests that small agencies are more likely to have higher rates for all types of crime.

Parallel with the literature, all structural level predictors are positively associated with crime rates. Agencies having a higher percentage of renters in their jurisdictions are more likely to have higher property and total crime rates, but not violent crime rates. Communities with more African Americans have higher violent and total crime rates. Nevertheless, this finding is not valid for property crime rates. Among the structural level variables, only the percentage of the population between 18-24 years of age was consistently found to be insignificant in predicting crime rates.

In terms of community policing variables, the training and problem-solving dimension is the only positive significant predictor for all type of crime rates.

Large Agency Model for Property Crime Rates

The first three hypotheses which state that an increase in the level of implementation of community policing will result in a reduction in property, violent, and total crime rates respectively are also tested for the large agency sample.

In terms of departmental control variables, only police size has a significant positive impact on property crime rates. This suggests that agencies which have a greater number of officers per 1,000 residents are more likely to have higher property crime rates.

The model illustrates that the percentage of urbanized area, the percentage of the population between 18 and 24 years of age, the percentage of residents living below the poverty level, and the percentage of divorced males have a significant positive effect on property crime rates. Conversely, "single female headed households living with children under 17 years of age", "renters", and "African Americans" are not significant predictors of property crime rates.

Table 18

Large Agency Regression Model for Property Crime Rates

Variable	Coefficient	Beta	t
Police Size[2]	13.949***	.513	19.071
COP Officers[3]	.042	.024	1.095
Education[4] Requirement	1.944	.033	1.505
Urbanized Area[3]	.329***	.231	8.419
Single Female Households[3]	.384	.043	1.021
Renters[3]	-.106	-.051	-1.531
18-24 Years of Age[3]	.578***	.098	3.572
Below Poverty[3]	.472**	.118	3.008
Divorced Males[3]	6.462***	.258	11.592
African American[3]	-.065	-.041	-1.261
Community Contribution[1]	.089	.014	.593
Training & Problem-Solving[1]	.879***	.115	4.234
Problem-Solving Partnership[1]	-.292	-.037	-1.486
Constant	-63.803***		-15.655
R^2 = .615 F = 106.566 S_e = 15.49393 n = 881			

Note: *** $p < .001$, ** $p < .01$, * $p < .05$

Like the full models, training and problem-solving is the only dimension of community policing activity that reached statistical significance. It suggests that those agencies which implement training and problem-solving activities to a greater extent are more likely to have higher property crime rates.

The variables "police size", "divorced males", "urbanized area", and "people living below the poverty level" respectively make the strongest unique contribution to predicting property crime rates when other variables in the model are controlled. The model itself explained roughly 61% of the variance in the property crime rates. The R^2 value illustrates that the model is a better predictor of property crime rates for the large agency sub-sample.

Large Agency Model for Violent Crime Rates

This section reports the testing of the second hypothesis, which states that if the level of implementation of community policing increases, violent crime rates will decrease. Results depicted in Table 19 illustrate that agencies with a higher number of police officers per 1,000 residents have higher violent crime rates. However, the percentage of community policing officers and the education requirements of agencies do not have any significant effect on violent crime rates.

In terms of structural level variables, the analysis reveals that the percentage of urbanized area, the percentage of single female headed households with children under 17 years of age, the percentage of the population between 18-24 years of age, and the percentage of divorced males all have significant positive effects on violent crime rates. Interestingly, the variable "renters", which is not significant in the property crime rates model, is significant in violent crime rates model. In contrast to the literature and other models' findings, agencies having a higher percentage of renters in their jurisdictions are more likely to have lower violent crime rates. Additionally, the percentage of the population living below the poverty level is insignificant for violent crime rates while it is significant in the property crime rates model.

The problem-solving partnership dimension of community policing has a negative effect on violent crime rates. This is consistent with the study's hypotheses which state that increases in the level of implementation of community policing activities result in lower crime rates. Nevertheless, the training and problem solving dimension of community policing has a positive significant effect on violent crime rates. The training and problem-solving dimension is a stronger predictor than the problem-solving partnership dimension. These findings are surprising because they suggest a contrasting directional effect based on the type (dimension) of community policing activity. Agencies which have partnerships or problem-solving partnership agreements with more community groups are more likely to have lower levels of violent crime rates. Conversely, agencies which train their personnel and citizens in community policing and use a variety of problem-solving techniques are more likely to have higher violent crime rates. Overall, this model explains 61% of the variance in violent crime rates. The strongest unique contributors are "police size", "single female headed households with children under 17 years of age", "divorced males", and "renters" respectively.

Table 19
Large Agency Regression Model for Violent Crime Rates

Variable	Coefficient	Beta	t
Police Size[2]	6.755***	.513	19.042
COP Officers[3]	.026	.031	1.428
Education[4] Requirement	.231	.008	.368
Urbanized Area[3]	.079***	.115	4.190
Single Female Households[3]	1.267***	.295	6.939
Renters[3]	-.133***	-.130	-3.941
18-24 Years of Age[3]	.321***	.112	4.087
Below Poverty[3]	.131	.067	1.720
Divorced Males[3]	2.516***	.207	9.306
African American[3]	-.025	-.033	-.121
Community Contribution[1]	.009	.003	.904

Table 19
Large Agency Regression Model for Violent Crime Rates (Cond't)

Training & Problem-Solving[1]	.417***	.113	4.140
Problem-Solving Partnership[1]	-.233*	-.060	-2.447
Constant	-26.828***		-13.571
$R^2 = .615$ F = 106.689 $S_e = 7.51539$ n = 881			

Note: *** $p < .001$, ** $p < .01$, * $p < .05$

Large Agency Model for Total Crime Rates

The third hypothesis states that if the level of implementation of community policing increases, total crime rates will decrease. Similar to the property and violent crime rates model, "police size" is the only significant predictor among other departmental control variables (the education requirement and the percentage of community policing officers). Agencies which have more police officers are more likely to have higher total crime rates.

In terms of structural variables, this model differs from the violent crime rates model in only one variable, the percentage of the population living below the poverty level. This predictor becomes significant in this model. The percentage of African Americans in the population is insignificant for all models for large agency sub-samples. The percentage of renters, like in the violent crime rates model, has a negative impact on total crime rates suggesting the higher the percentage of renters, the lower the crime rates. The variables, "urbanized area", "single female headed households with children under 17 years of age", "population between 18-24 years of age", "population below poverty", and "divorced males" are all significant and positively associated with total crime rates.

Two dimensions of community policing have a contrasting directional impact on total crime rates similar to the violent crime rates model. The more an agency implements community policing activities related to problem-solving partnership, the lower the crime rates. On the other hand, agencies which implement a training and problem–solving dimension of community policing to a greater extent are more likely to have higher total crime rates. The predictors in the model account for roughly 66% of the variance in total crime rates. The four strongest unique contributors are "police size", "divorced males", "urbanized area", and "single female headed households with children under 17 years of age respectively

Table 20
Large Agency Regression Model for Total Crime Rates

Variable	Coefficient	Beta	t
Police Size[2]	20.704***	.537	21.245
COP Officers[3]	.068	.027	1.341
Education[4] Requirement	2.175	.026	1.263
Urbanized Area[3]	.409***	.202	7.844
Single Female Households[3]	1.652**	.131	3.292
Renters[3]	-.239*	-.080	-2.583
18-24 Years of Age[3]	.898***	.107	4.168
Below Poverty[3]	.603**	.106	2.883
Divorced Males[3]	8.979***	.252	12.088

Table 20
Large Agency Regression Model for Total Crime Rates (Cond't)

African American[3]	-.091	.069	-1.315
Community Contribution[1]	.080	.009	.401
Training & Problem-Solving[1]	1.295***	.120	4.685
Problem-Solving Partnership[1]	-.525*	-.046	-2.006
Constant	-90.631***		-16.990
R^2 = .661 F = 129.921 S_e = 20.644189 n = 881			

Note: *** $p < .001$, ** $p < .01$, * $p < .05$

Summary of Findings for Large Agency Model

In each of the large agency models, the percentage of community policing officers, the education requirement for new recruits, the percentage of African Americans, and the community contribution dimension of community policing did not reach statistical significance.

Within the exception of two variables (percentage of renters and percentage of African Americans), all structural level predictors are positively associated with each type of crime rate. In contrast to the literature, agencies having a higher percentage of renters in their jurisdictions are more likely to have lower violent and total crime rates. However, this finding is not consistent with property crime rates. Agencies having a higher percentage of single female headed households with children under 17 years of age are more likely to have higher violent and total crime rates, but not property crime rates. The percentage of people living below the poverty level is an insignificant predictor of violent crime rates, but a significant predictor of property and total crime rates.

Consistent with the full models, the training and problem-solving dimension of community policing has a positive impact on all type of crime rates. In support of the study's hypotheses which state that an increase in the level of implementation of community policing will result in a reduction in crime rates, the problem-solving partnership dimension of community policing has a negative impact on violent and total crime rates, but not on property crime rates.

Small Agency Model for Property Crime Rates

This section tests the hypothesis which states that if the level of implementation of community policing increases, property crime rates will decrease in the small agency sample. In terms of departmental control variables, only the variable "police size" has a positive impact on property crime rates. These findings suggest that agencies which have a greater number of officers per 1,000 residents are more likely to have higher property crime rates. However, the percentage of community policing officers and the education requirement for new recruits did not reach statistical significance.

The model illustrates that the variables "urbanized area", "single female headed households", "renters", "population living below the poverty level", and "divorced males" have a significant positive effect on property crime rates. Conversely, the variables "youth between 18-24 years of age" and "African Americans" are insignificant predictors.

Consistent with the findings of the full models, training and problem-solving is the only dimension of community policing activity that reached statistical significance. These findings suggest that agencies which implement training and problem-solving activities to a greater extent are more likely to have higher property crime rates.

The variables "police size", "urbanized area", "training and problem solving and "divorced males" respectively make the strongest unique contribution to predicting property crime rates when other variables in the model are controlled. The model itself explained roughly 41% of the variance in the property crime rates.

Table 21
Small Agency Regression Model for Property Crime Rates

Variable	Coefficient	Beta	t
Police Size[2]	4.518***	.350	16.856
COP Officers[3]	-.032	-034	-1.655
Education[4] Requirement	.787	.011	.532
Urbanized Area[3]	.167***	.252	9.951
Single Female Households[3]	.846**	.109	3.030
Renters[3]	.236**	.114	3.734
18-24 Years of Age[3]	-.057	-.011	-.467
Below Poverty[3]	.253*	.077	2.369
Divorced Males[3]	2.463***	.134	6.086
African American[3]	.031	.019	.646
Community Contribution[1]	.309	.033	1.507
Training & Problem-Solving[1]	1.449***	.170	6.481
Problem-Solving Partnership[1]	.028	.003	.113
Constant	-25.587***		10.525
$R^2 = .409$ $F = 80.202$ $S_e = 20.35174$ $n = 1,521$			

Note: *** $p < .001$, ** $p < .01$, * $p < .05$

Small Agency Model for Violent Crime Rates

In this section, the hypothesis which states that if the level of implementation of community policing increases, violent crime rates will decrease is tested. Results depicted in Table 22 illustrate that agencies with a greater number of police officers per 1,000 residents have higher violent crime rates. The education requirement and the percentage of community policing officers are significantly associated with violent crime rates.

In terms of structural level variables, this model differs from the previous one. The percentage of urbanized area, the percentage of single female headed households with children under 17 years of age, the percentage of people living below the poverty level, and the percentage of divorced males have significant positive effects; whereas, the percentage of renters does not have any significant effect on violent crime rates.

Table 22
Small Agency Regression Model for Violent Crime Rates

Variable	Coefficient	Beta	t
Police Size[2]	1.320***	.206	9.653
COP Officers[3]	-.006	-.014	-.640
Education[4] Requirement	.557	.016	-.131
Urbanized Area[3]	.066***	.200	7.703
Single Female Households[3]	.839***	.217	5.889
Renters[3]	.058	.056	1.790
18-24 Years of Age[3]	-.027	-.011	-.432
Below Poverty[3]	.210***	.129	3.854
Divorced Males[3]	1.368***	.150	6.625
African American[3]	.059*	.073	2.438
Community Contribution[1]	-.082	-.018	-.782
Training & Problem-Solving[1]	.732***	.173	6.421
Problem-Solving Partnership[1]	.073	.014	.569
Constant	-.14.694***		-11.846
R^2 = .377 F = 70.049 S_e = 10.38399 n = 1,521			

Note: *** $p < .001$, ** $p < .01$, * $p < .05$

In addition, the percentage of African Americans reached statistical significance. The higher the percentage of African Americans in the community, the higher the violent crime rate is.

Training and problem-solving is the only dimension of community policing activity that has a positive significant impact on violent crime rates. Overall, this model explains 38% of the variance in violent crime rates. The strongest unique contributors are "police size", "urbanized area", "training and problem solving", and "divorced males" respectively.

Small Agency Model for Total Crime Rates

This section tests the hypothesis, if the level of implementation of community policing increases, total crime rates will decrease. Like the property and violent crime rates model, "police size" is the only significant predictor among the departmental control variables. Agencies which have more police officers are more likely to have higher total crime rates. The two variables, the education requirement and the percentage of community policing officers are not significantly associated with violent crime rates.

In terms of significant structural level factors, this model is the same as the property crime rates model. The variables "urbanized area", "single female headed households with children under 17 years of age", "renters", "population living below the poverty level", and "divorced males" have a significant positive effect on total crime rates. On the other hand, the percentage of youth between 18-24 years of age and the percentage of African Americans in the population are insignificant structural level factors.

Like the two other models, training and problem-solving is the only dimension of community policing activity that is significant. These findings suggest that agencies which implement training and problem-solving activities to a greater extent are more likely to have higher total crime rates.

The variables "police size", "urbanized area", "training and problem solving and "single female headed households with children under 17" respectively make the strongest unique contribution to predicting total crime rates when other variables in the model are controlled. The model itself explained roughly 44% of the variance in total crime rates.

Table 23

Small Agency Regression Model for Total Crime Rates

Variable	Coefficient	Beta	t
Police Size[2]	5.838***	.321	15.816
COP Officers[3]	-.038	-.029	-1.446
Education[4] Requirement	.231	.002	.113
Urbanized Area[3]	.232***	.250	10.079
Single Female Households[3]	1.684***	.154	4.382
Renters[3]	.294**	.100	3.375
18-24 Years of Age[3]	-.084	-.012	-.499
Below Poverty[3]	.463**	.101	3.148
Divorced Males[3]	3.031***	.148	6.874
African American[3]	.090	.039	1.372
Community Contribution[1]	.227	.017	.804
Training & Problem-Solving[1]	2.182***	.182	.293
Problem-Solving Partnership[1]	.101	.007	.293
Constant	-40.281		-12.031
R^2 = .436 F = 89.477 S_e = 28.028142 n = 1,521			

Note: *** p < .001, ** p < .01, * p < .05

Summary of Findings for Small Agency Models

In each of the small agency models, the education requirement for new recruits, the percentage of community policing officers, the percentage of the population between 18-24 years of age, and the community contribution and problem-solving partnership dimensions of community policing never reached statistical significance.

Agencies which have a higher percentage of renters in their jurisdictions are more likely to have higher property and total crime rates. However, this finding is not significant for violent crime rates. The percentage of African Americans has a positive significant effect only on violent crime rates. All other significant structural level predictors (urbanized area, single female headed households with children under 17 years of age, population below poverty, and divorced males) also have positive effects on crime rates.

As full models, only the training and problem-solving dimension of community policing is a significant predictor for each type of crime rate which suggests that agencies which implement training and problem-solving activities to a greater extent are more likely to have higher rates of each type of crime.

Comparison Models

It is hypothesized that the effect of the level of implementation of community policing on crime rates differs according to the agency size. There are some differences between large and small agencies in terms of the effect of an independent variable. These are illustrated in the separate models discussed above. Are these differences significant? Does the effect of a predictor variable depend on another variable (in this case agency size)?

Comparison Model for Property Crime Rates

This section reports on the test of the fourth hypothesis which states that there is a difference between large and small agencies in terms of the effect of community policing variables on property crime rates. Interaction effects are identified for the variables "police size", "urbanized area", "renters", "population between 18-24 years of age", and "divorced males". Their effects differ based on agency size. Among these variables, "police size", "urbanized area", and "divorced males" have significant positive effects on property crime rates for both large.

Table 24

Comparison Model for Property Crime Rates

Variable	Large Agencies		Small Agencies		
	b	S.E	b	S.E	Z
Police Size[2]	13.949***	.731	4.518***	.268	**12.140**
COP Officers[3]	.042	.038	-.032	.019	.026
Education[4] Requirement	1.944	1.292	.787	1.480	.589
Urbanized Area[3]	.329***	.039	.167***	.017	**8.526**
Single Female Households[3]	.384	.377	.846**	.279	.987
Renters[3]	-.106	.069	.236**	.063	**-3.842**
18-24 Years of Age[3]	.578***	.162	-.057	.122	**2.579**
Below Poverty[3]	.472**	.157	.253*	.107	1.164
Divorced Males[3]	6.462***	.557	2.463***	.405	**5.812**
African American[3]	-.065	.052	.031	.048	-1.476
Community Contribution[1]	.089	.150	.309	.205	.343
Training & Problem-Solving[1]	.879***	.207	1.449***	.224	-1.88
Problem-Solving Partnership[1]	-.292	.196	.028	.251	-1.032
	$R^2 = .615$ F = 106.566 $S_e = $ 15.4939 n = 881		$R^2 = .409$ F = 80.202 $S_e = $ 20.3517 n = 1,521		

Note: *** $p < .001$, ** $p < .01$, * $p < .05$

and small agencies, but the effects on large agencies are more pronounced. An increase in any of these variables is likely to result in an increase in property crime rates.

The effect of the percentage of renters and the percentage of the population between 18-24 years of age are also moderated by agency size; however, the direction of their association with property crime rates is different for large and small agencies. Specifically, small agencies which have a higher percentage of renters are more likely to have higher property crime rates than large agencies. Large agencies which have a greater percentage of the population between 18-24 years of age are more likely to have higher property crime rates than small agencies.

With regard to the community policing variables, the z-test score did not reach statistical significance. The training and problem solving dimension has a positive impact on property crime rates for both large and small departments; and this impact is equal for both groups.

Comparison Model for Violent Crime Rates

The fifth hypothesis which states there is a difference between large and small agencies in terms of the effect of community policing variables on violent crime rates is tested in this section. Interaction effects are identified for "police size", "the percentage of community policing officers", "population between 18-24 years of age", "divorced males", "African Americans", and "the training and problem-solving" variables which suggest their effects differ based on an agency's size. Among these variables, "police size", "divorced males", and "training and problem-solving" have significant positive effects on violent crime rates for both large and small agencies. The effects of police size and the percentage of divorced males are more prominent for large agencies; whereas, the effect of the training and problem solving dimension of community policing is more prominent for small agencies. Large agencies which have a higher percentage of divorced males and more officers per 1,000 residents are more likely to have higher violent crime rates. On the other hand, small agencies which implement the training and problem solving dimensions of community policing to a greater extent are more likely to have higher violent crime rates than large agencies.

The effect of the percentage of the population between 18-24 years of age is also moderated by agency size. It has a positive significant effect on violent crime rates for large agencies; whereas, its effect is negative and insignificant for small agencies. That is, large agencies which have a higher percentage of population between 18-24 years of age are more likely to have higher violent crime rates than small agencies. The impact of the percentage of African Americans differs based on agency size. Small agencies which have a higher percentage of African Americans in the population are more likely to have higher violent crime rates than large agencies.

The findings suggest that the percentage of community policing officers is insignificant. However, the effect differs based on the agency size, suggesting that small agencies having a higher percentage of community policing officers are more likely to have lower violent crime rates.

Table 25

Comparison Model for Violent Crime Rates

Variable	Large Agencies		Small Agencies		
	b	S.E	b	S.E	Z
Police Size[2]	6.755***	.335	1.320***	.137	**15.055**
COP Officers[3]	.026	.018	-.006	.010	**2.514**
Education[4] Requirement	.231	.627	-.557	.755	-.332
Urbanized Area[3]	.079***	.019	.066***	.009	.684
Single Female Households[3]	1.267***	.183	.839***	.142	.230
Renters[3]	-.133***	.034	.058	.032	-.044
18-24 Years of Age[3]	.321***	.078	-.027	.062	**2.060**
Below Poverty[3]	.131	.076	.210***	.055	-.887
Divorced Males[3]	2.516***	.270	1.368***	.206	**3.396**
African American[3]	-.025	.025	.059*	.024	**-2.470**

Table 25
Comparison Model for Violent Crime Rates (Cond't)

Community Contribution[1]	.009	.073	-.082	.105	-.507
Training & Problem-Solving[1]	.417***	.101	.732***	.114	**-2.086**
Problem-Solving Partnership[1]	-.233*	.095	.073	.128	-.1.92
	$R^2 = .615$ F = 106.689 S_e = 7.51539 n = 881		$R^2 = .377$ F = 70.049 S_e = 10.3839 n =1,521		

Note: *** $p < .001$, ** $p < .01$, * $p < .05$

Comparison Model for Total Crime Rates

The last hypothesis which states there is a difference between large and small agencies in terms of the effect of community policing variables on total crime rates was tested in this section. Interaction effects are identified for police size, the percentage of urbanized area, renters, the percentage of the population between 18-24 years of age, the percentage of African Americans, the percentage of divorced males, and the training and problem-solving dimension of community policing. Their effects differ based on agency size. Among these variables, "police size", "urbanized area", and "divorced males" have significant positive effects on total crime rates for both large and small agencies, but the effects on large agencies are more pronounced. An increase in any of these variables is likely to result in an increase in total crime rates.

The effect of the percentage of renters and the percentage of the population between 18-24 years of age are also moderated by agency size; however, the direction of their association with total crime rates is different for large and small agencies. In small agencies, having a higher percentage of renters is associated with higher total crime rates; whereas, in large agencies, having a higher percentage of renters is associated with lower total crime rates. In large agencies, a higher percentage of the population between 18-24 years of age is associated with higher total crime rates; whereas, in small agencies a higher percentage of the population between 18-24 years of age is associated with lower total crime rates.

Despite the fact that the variable "African Americans" is insignificant, it interacts with agency size. The directions of the relationships with total crime rates are contrasting. That is, a higher percentage of African Americans in the population is associated with lower total crime rates in large agencies, yet it is associated with higher total crime rates in small agencies.

With regard to the community policing variables, the z-test score for problem-solving partnership did not reach statistical significance. This suggests that the effect of this variable is the same for both groups. However, the regression model which includes only large agencies reveals that the problem-solving partnership is associated with lower violent and total crime rates. The training and problem solving dimension has a significant positive impact on total crime rates for both large and small departments, and this impact is more pronounced for small agencies.

Table 26

Comparison Model for Total Crime Rates

Variable	Large Agencies		Small Agencies		
	b	S.E	B	S.E	Z
Police Size[2]	20.704***	.975	5.838***	.369	**14.266**
COP Officers[3]	.068	.051	-.038	.026	.058
Education[4] Requirement	2.175	1.722	.231	2.038	1.119
Urbanized Area[3]	.409***	.052	.232***	.023	**3.54**
Single Female Households[3]	1.652**	.502	1.684***	.384	-.050
Renters[3]	-.239*	.092	.294**	.087	**-4.298**
18-24 Years of Age[3]	.898***	.216	-.084	.167	**3.003**
Below Poverty[3]	.603**	.209	.463**	.147	.551
Divorced Males[3]	8.979***	.743	3.831***	.557	**5.547**

Table 26

Comparison Model for Total Crime Rates (Cont't)

African American[3]	-.091	.069	.090	.066	**-1.989**
Community Contribution[1]	.080	.201	.227	.283	-.424
Training & Problem-Solving[1]	1.295***	.276	2.182***	.308	**-2.147**
Problem-Solving Partnership[1]	-.525*	.262	.101	.346	-1.445
	$R^2 = .661$ $F = 129.921$ $S_e = 20.64418$ $n = 881$		$R^2 = .436$ $F = 89.477$ $S_e = 28.02814$ $n = 1,521$		

Note: *** $p < .001$, ** $p < .01$, * $p < .05$

Summary of Differences among the Models

This section discusses the differences in the models. As Table 27 illustrates, several variables have consistent positive effects on the dependent variables for each model. These variables are: "police size", "urbanized area", "divorced males", and "training and problem-solving". This finding suggests that agencies which have more officers per 1,000 residents, serve a jurisdiction having a more urbanized area, and have a higher percentage of divorced males are more likely to have higher crime rates. In addition, contrary to the study's hypotheses, a higher degree of implementation of community policing results in higher crime rates. However, this finding is only valid for the training and problem-solving dimension of community policing.

The variable "agency size", which is included only for full models, consistently shows a significant negative impact suggesting that small agencies are more likely to have higher crime rates. The percentage of community policing officers and the community contribution dimension of community policing demonstrated that there is no significant relationship between crime rates for all the models. These findings suggest that these variables are not good predictors for the regression models.

According to the literature, structural variables are known correlates of crime. Since the focus of this book is to examine the effect of the level of implementation of community policing on crime rates, no hypothesis was constructed regarding the effects of structural level variables. However, it is noteworthy to briefly examine their effects. For example, two of these variables (urbanized area and divorced males) consistently make the strongest unique contributions to predicting crime rates for almost all of the models. The percentage of single female headed households with children under 17 is also positively associated with crime rates for all models, with the exception of property crime rates for large agencies. The percentage of the population living below the poverty level has significant positive relationships with crime rates for all models, except violent crime rates for large agencies.

Not surprisingly, some of these variables differ for each model. For example, the percentage of African Americans is a significant predictor in only three models (full models' violent crime rates and total crime rates, and in the small agency's model violent crime rates). Interestingly, the percentage of African Americans does not appear to have a significant effect on crime rates for any large agency models. The percentage of the population between 18 and 24 years of age is a significant predictor of crime rates in only large agency models. Lastly, the percentage of renters although significant, has a contrasting directional relationship with crime rates. Analyses reveal that the percentage of renters has a positive relationship with property and total crime rates for the full and the small agency models; but it has a negative relationship with violent crime rates and total crime rates in the large agency models.

Among the three departmental control variables, police size is the only consistent predictor that has a positive effect on crime for each type of crime rate. Having an officer with a college degree or some college credits has a positive significant effect on property and total crime rates only in the full models.

With regard to the effect of the level of implementation of community policing, the problem-solving partnership variable illustrates the hypothesized effects on violent and total crime rates for only large agencies, At this point, it is important to demonstrate the merit of choosing to include three dimensions as measures of level of implementation of community policing instead of using a single summated index. When models include a summated index of community policing as a unidimensional construct instead of three separate dimensions, community policing appears to have a significant positive impact on crime rates. There is only one exceptional model (large agencies' violent crime rates). For this model which separately utilizes three dimensions of community policing, a problem solving partnership has a significant negative effect; and training and problem-solving has a significant positive effect. When the community policing summated index is replaced with three separate community policing variables in the model, the community policing index turns out to be insignificant. In short, the two opposite directional significant community policing variables cancel out their effects when they are combined into a single variable.

In fact, if the summated index had been selected for the analyses, the hypothesized effect of problem-solving partnership on violent and total crime rates in large agencies would not have been observed. Furthermore, by using three dimensions, only training and problem-solving type of community policing activities (not other types) were consistently found to have a significant positive impact on crime rates.

Table 27

The Unstandardized Regression Coefficients for Each Model

Variable	Model								
	Full Property	Full Violent	Full Total	Large Property	Large Violent	Large Total	Small Property	Small Violent	Small Total
Police Size	5.301***	1.735***	7.036***	13.949***	6.755***	20.704***	4.518***	1.320***	5.838***
COP Officers	-.025	-.004	-.029	.042	.025	.068	-.032	-.006	-.038
Education Requirement	2.590*	.297	2.888*	1.944	.231	2.175	.787	-.557	.231
Agency Size	-3.068**	-1.500**	-4.568**	-	-	-	-	-	-
Urbanized Area	.197***	.075***	.272***	.329***	.079***	.409***	.167***	.066***	.232***
Single female households	.652**	.896***	1.548***	.384	1.267***	1.652**	.846**	.839***	1.684***
Renters	.188***	.020	.208**	-.106	-.133***	-.239*	.236**	.058	.294**
Population 18-24 years of age	.050	.029	.079	.578***	.321***	.898***	-.057	-.027	-.084
Population below poverty	.365***	.236***	.601***	.472**	.13	.603**	.253*	.210***	.463**
Divorced Males	3.432***	1.690***	5.123***	6.462***	2.516***	8.979***	2.463***	1.368***	3.831***

Table 27

The Unstandardized Regression Coefficients for Each Model (Cond't)

African American Population	.058	.066***	.124*	-.065	-.025	-.091	.031	.059*	.090
Community Contribution	.229	-.044	.184	.089	.009	.080	.309	-.082	.227
Training & Problem-solving	1.435***	.703***	.703***	.879***	.417***	1.295***	1.449***	.732***	2.182***
Problem-solving Partnership	-.099	-.053	-.152	-.292	-.233*	-.525*	.028	.073	.101

Note: *** p < .001, ** p < .01, * p < .05

CHAPTER 6

What We Learned

OPERATIONALIZATION OF COMMUNITY POLICING

Research on community policing is inherently limited due to the absence of valid and reliable measures of community policing. The problematic nature of the theoretical framework generates a variety of conceptual and operational level definitions of community policing, which, in turn, might cause community policing research to reveal inconsistent results. Bayley (1994) asserted that the success of community policing is very difficult to evaluate because its meaning varies according to each person.

Previous studies using the LEMAS community policing section to operationalize community policing employed different approaches such as creating a summated index of all or a few variables, or creating a subgroup of community policing activities. This study utilized factor analysis to uncover the latent structure, and generated reliable scales as measures of the level of implementation of community policing.

Limited by secondary data, results indicated that using three scales each representing a dimension of community policing was a better analysis strategy than using a summated index of all variables in the LEMAS community policing section. The three scale strategy enabled the researcher to identify which dimension and related activities had a significant impact on crime rates. This approach is also supported by previous research. Cheurprakobkit (2002) contended that some dimensions of community policing are emphasized more than other components in practice; therefore, it is important to separately analyze the effect of each dimension. The different effects among the types of community policing activities would not have been explored had the summated index been utilized. For example, community contribution (surveying citizens and using this information for various departmental activities) was not a significant predictor of crime rates; whereas, the training and problem-solving dimension consistently demonstrated a significant positive relationship with crime rates.

When a summated index is included in the regression models, results indicated that the level of implementation of community policing is positively associated with crime rates for almost all models. With this methodology, a substantial finding that indicates surveying citizens and having a problem-solving partnership do not have any significant impact on crime rates would not be captured.

REGRESSION FINDINGS

It was hypothesized that an increase in the level of implementation of community policing results in a decline in crime rates. Contextual and some departmental variables were used as control variables when the impact of the level of implementation of community policing was examined. However, it is observed that the relative importance of some of these control variables exceed the relative importance of explanatory (community policing) variables. Although no specific hypothesis was established for the effect of control variables, they are briefly discussed.

Departmental Factors

Agencies having more officers per 1,000 residents are more likely to have higher crime rates. This effect differs based on the agency size, suggesting the effect is more prominent for large agencies. This one variable, having more officers per 1,000 residents, makes the strongest unique contribution to predicting crime rates for all of the models. The results of studies on police size and its relationship to crime are ambiguous in terms of both the direction of the relationship and the temporal ordering of the effects (Eck & Maguire, 2000; Levitt, 1997; Marvel & Moody 1996). For some, crime rates affect the police size; for others, police size affects crime rates. In some samples, there is a reciprocal relationship between the two (Loftin & McDowall, 1998). In addition, it was suggested that social economic factors are far more powerful determinants of crime than the number of police (Sherman & Eck, 2006). It was found that police size was the most powerful variable in predicting crime rates when structural level variables were controlled. However, given the requirements of casual validity, it cannot be claimed that an increase in the number of police results in higher crime rates. Two explanations seem plausible when interpreting why the impact of police size is the strongest, and why this impact is more prominent for large agencies.

First, more officers might increase the size of the beats to be patrolled as well as the frequency of the patrol sequence; hence, more officers might discover more crime. Second, as Marvel and Moody (1996) suggested, increasing the number of officers in big cities is more effective than additional officers in small cities because the amount of crime is greater in large cities (p. 632). For small cities, it might be the case that there is a tipping point for the effectiveness of number of police officers. After reaching this point, putting additional police officers on streets does not affect crime rates.

The percentage of community policing officers has a negative relationship with crime rates in both the full and small agency models; whereas, it has a positive relationship in large agency models. Clearly, these effects never reach significance in any models. Community policing might be only cosmetic for many agencies (Bayley, 1996; Walker & Katz, 2005). For example, an agency might announce that all of its officers are community policing officers, yet how these officers police their communities might not be that different than traditional policing. It is a matter of the quality, not the quantity. To be successful, community policing has to be embraced and implemented by both rank and file officers. It also requires an organizational change from the top down (White, 2007). However, the police subculture or resistance to change has to be addressed in this process. It is difficult, and requires time, even in agencies managed by innovative police chiefs. In that sense, one possible explanation for a lack of significance may be due to the resistance from mid-level supervisors and file officers. Therefore, the objectives determined by the top administration may not be reflected in street-level policing (Vito et al., 2005; Zhao et al., 1995).

In addition, simply allocating more officers for community policing does not guarantee its implementation. It is likely that community policing is a form of symbolic politics for better public relations and political gains (Reed, 1999). Police chiefs who want to appear innovative declare that their agencies have a higher percentage of community policing officers, when, in fact, they do not do anything different than traditional policing. Without additional and detailed information, counting the number of community policing officers cannot provide meaningful results for interpretation purposes.

Higher education is expected to provide better police performance and effective policing (Chappell, Lanza-Kaduce, & Johnston, 2005; MacDonald, 2002; Stevens, 2003). In the early 1900s, August Vollmer emphasized the importance of college education and became the first chief in the nation to provide higher education to police officers. However, subsequent law enforcement agencies were not able to institute Vollmer's initiative. Tremendous variation in recruitment and training standards was evident even in the 1990s (Marion, 1998). This study's findings indicate that among the sample of 2,402 agencies in the U.S., only 19% of them required some college credits or a college degree for new recruits. This sample includes all law enforcement agencies in the U.S having more than 100 sworn officers. The majority of the agencies recruits and employs new officers with only a high school diploma. Police officers having higher educational level are more likely to be open to innovative policing strategies. Although weak, correlations are positive between components of community policing and an education requirement (Table 14).

In this book, the effect of an education requirement reaches significance only in the full model for property and total crime rates. This finding suggests that agencies having more officers with some college credits or a college degree are more likely to have higher property and total crime rates. MacDonald (2002) also found that there was no consistent effect of a college degree on violent crime rates. It is difficult to interpret this finding when the expected direction is negative, and its positive effect is only significant in the full models. One possible explanation might be that officers with a college degree are more sensitive to crime and crime reporting than other officers. These potentially younger and college educated officers might tend to report even trivial property crimes that might have been traditionally ignored by other officers. This, in turn, can result in an increase in reported property crime.

Agency size as an independent variable was only used in the full models. It was observed that small agencies are more likely to have more crimes per 1,000 residents. In addition, it is hypothesized that the effect of community policing differs based on an agency's size. Through the comparison models, the second group of three hypotheses is tested along with the possible interaction effects. Analyses illustrate that not only the effect of community policing variables, but also the effect of contextual and departmental control variables differed for small and large agencies.

If eliminating police-community alienation is the first priority of community policing, one might perceive community policing as a strategy for large city police departments where a sense of community and community-police relations are likely to be weak. Nevertheless, parallel to this study's findings, several scholars have found that community policing had an impact on crime even in small agencies (Brand & Birzer, 2003; Cordner & Scarborough, 2003; Wells & Weisheit, 2004; Zhao et al., 2002; Zhao & Thurman, 2003). These studies' findings also illustrate that crime is not a uniform phenomenon in the U.S.

Osgood and Chambers (2000) argued that social disorganization theory has been rarely examined in small communities. This book did not test social disorganization theory, but related variables such as urbanized area, single female headed households with children under 17, and poverty were identified as significant predictors of crime rates for both small and large cities at different levels. These results also support Wells' & Weisheit's (2004) argument that contextual variables are influential for crime rates even in very rural areas. Consequently, it can be said that both community policing and contextual variables influenced crime rates even in small agencies, and the direction and strength of this influence differ based on the agency's size.

Structural Level Factors

Communities dominated by high residential mobility, population density, economic disadvantage, and disrupted families are associated with higher crime rates (Shaw & McKay, 1942; Sampson & Grove, 1989). In the same way, the community policing literature suggests that community characteristics play a more significant role than any type of community policing activity (Bowling and Foster, 2002). Rosenbaum and Lurigio (1994) argued that the ability of community policing to reduce crime has not been proved particularly in inner-city urban areas where it was deemed to be most effective. In support of these contentions, this study's findings indicate that contextual variables are more important predictors of crime while controlling for the characteristics of a law enforcement agency. This does not mean that statistical models in this book included all relevant characteristics of an agency. The explained variations (the highest was 66%) of the models indicated that at least 34% of the variation needs to be explained by other relevant variables that were not included. These variables might be related to other departmental factors or a different policing strategy as well as other contextual variables.

Consistent in all models, the percentage of urbanized area, divorced males, single female headed households with children under 17, and people living below the poverty level are positively associated with crime rates. These findings are supported by previous research. Young people, men, economically disadvantaged people, and urban residents are more likely to be associated with crime (Heimer & Coster 1999; Markowitz & Felson, 1998). However, the percentage of African Americans, the percentage of the population between 18 and 24 years of age, and the percentage of renters yielded inconsistent results. There is a positive association between the percentage of African Americans and violent crime rates in both the small agency and the full models. This effect is more prominent in small communities. It is likely that even a one percent increase in the African American population makes a more substantial difference on crime rates in small communities than in large communities which most likely already have a significant proportion of African Americans in their population.

Based on an examination of 164 big cities (population greater than 250,000), MacDonald (2002) did not find any significant relationship between the percentage of youth between 18-24 years of age and violent crime rates. However, in the large agency models, the current study found that jurisdictions having a higher percentage of youth between 18-24 years of age are more likely to have higher crime rates. There are two possible explanations why this variable is a significant factor in only large agencies. First, in small cities, informal social control might be preferred over formal social control. Instead of referring delinquent youth to the formal justice system, small communities might more frequently use informal mechanisms to deal with delinquency. Second, opportunities for crime might be greater while the likelihood of apprehension might be reduced in larger communities. Alternatively, the effects of other variables such as the percentage of renters and African Americans in the population might suppress the effect of this variable in the small agency models.

The percentage of renters is negatively associated with violent and total crime rates in the large agency model, but it is positively associated with property and total crime rates in the full and small agency models. Renters were used as a proxy measure for residential mobility. Previous studies found a positive relationship between the percentage of renters and crime rates (Duman, 2007; Zhao et al., 2002).

The full models in this book manifest this positive relationship; however, the negative relationship identified for large agencies was difficult to interpret without additional data regarding individual and cultural differences among communities. The plausible explanation might be that since residentially unstable people are less integrated within the community in which they live, they might be more indifferent to what occurs in the neighborhood, and they might not be as likely to report crimes to the police (Sampson, Raudenbush, & Earls, 1997).

Community Policing Factors

Three different variables were utilized to measure the extent of implementation of community policing in an agency. The first composite measure, community contribution, never reached significance in any of the models. Community policing supporters suggested that collecting information from the public contributes to policing in two ways: First, police departments might better understand community needs and develop a community-based policing plan. Second, they can establish new goals and modify priorities for their departments (Kappeler & Gaines, 2005; Peak & Glensor, 2000).

Descriptive statistics indicate that agencies score the lowest on this dimension of community policing. Approximately 70% of the agencies score zero on this scale. In order for an agency to score on this dimension, it had to conduct a survey or sponsor a survey on various topics such as public satisfaction with police and/or public perception of crime. Furthermore, the agency had to use the survey information to assess and improve departmental activities. For example, results might influence the evaluation of officer performance and the reallocation of the patrol beat.

It is understandable why agencies do not favor surveys. Conducting surveys requires a considerable amount of time, money, and expertise. Chapman (2008) points to the need for expertise in research to administer surveys, analyze the data, and report on the results. Even agencies committed to community policing are likely to use less costly methods to solicit citizen input. For example, community meetings are easier and a less resource demanding way to facilitate community involvement. Are both ways of information gathering comparable in terms of quality? The obvious answer is no. However, conducting a survey or sponsoring a survey without any serious political pressure, scientific assistance, and funding is not feasible for most law enforcement agencies. Roth et al. (2004) found that between 1998 and 2000 citizen surveys were the least practiced technique for community partnership. Moreover, evaluation studies do not support the idea that collecting information from the community reduces crime (Wycoff & Skogan, 1993; Skogan, 2006). Consequently, it can be argued that the findings of the book regarding the effect of community contribution on crime rates are consistent with the literature.

The training and problem-solving dimension consistently shows a significant positive impact on crime rates in contrast to the study's hypotheses. In some models, it is one of the strongest unique predictors of crime rates. Given the study's design, it cannot be argued that this is a casual relationship. However, it is useful to consider why the results are in conflict with the study's hypotheses.

First, it is important to assess why training and problem-solving dimension is not related to crime reduction. Haberfeld (2002) contended that community policing training usually does not provide expected results in terms of the effective implementation of community policing. She argued that as a result of training, officers are not able to gain necessary skills such as effective communication and problem-solving that are vital in implementation of community policing. Second, training continues to place more emphasis on traditional policing rather than community policing. Therefore, for new recruits, the importance of community policing is underestimated. In addition, in the LEMAS survey questionnaire, the question that asks agencies about personnel training on community policing provides a cut-off point for training (a minimum of eight hours). For a strategy that requires an understanding of its philosophy and a radical change in the traditional police culture, an eight hour training requirement is clearly inadequate. Therefore, if a majority of agencies score on this dimension by providing very brief and superficial training, then it is quite likely that any crime reduction effect with community policing training will not be detected.

In terms of citizen education, there is one possible explanation why it does not result in any identifiable crime reduction effect. Perhaps the citizens who participated in these trainings are very likely to be the most police friendly citizens. Regardless of the education and training they received, they are likely to collaborate with law enforcement agencies. The rest of the citizens in the community who are likely to be the real targets (people who are the most distant from police) continue to refrain from getting involved in collaborative activities for creating safer communities.

There is considerable evidence that community policing, in practice, is more rhetoric than reality (Bayley, 1996; Reed, 1999, Weatheritt, 1988). Although agencies reported to the LEMAS that they implemented the various community policing activities, they might not undergo any change in their philosophy and/or organizational culture. Cordner and Biebel (2005) contended that even in a police department known as the nation's leader on problem-oriented policing, officers do very little different than traditional policing.

Once the possible explanations why training and problem-solving dimension does not work in the expected direction are addressed, the next concern is to present plausible reasons why it is associated with higher crime rates. With trained personnel and citizens, two-way communication might be significantly improved. Thus, more crime is reported. In this case, the actual incidence of crime committed in the same jurisdiction does not increase, however, as a result of improved interaction and communication, citizen crime reporting behavior might result in more crime reported to police. In support to this argument, Schnebly (2008) found that residents are more likely to report their victimization experiences to the police in the jurisdictions where agencies have a higher percentage of officers who have received community policing training. The same argument can be used in explaining the amplifying effect of problem-solving activities on crime rates. Increasing attention and sensitivity to crime related problems might lead agencies and citizens to detect more crime.

The problem-solving partnership dimension of community policing has a negative association with violent and total crime rates as hypothesized. However, this relationship is only significant for large agencies. An agency should have a written agreement or a problem-solving partnership with various community entities to score on this scale. In comparison with the community contribution dimension, the problem-solving partnership is more prevalent among agencies. Over 70% of the agencies have a written agreement or problem-solving partnership with at least one community entity. Tilley (2004) contended that without a problem-solving component, community policing is only expressive and ideological. The public ultimately demands a safe and problem-free environment from police departments. If a policing strategy does not perform better than traditional policing in terms of solving safety related problems, the public does not credit it as successful.

The crime prevention effect of a policing strategy is more likely to be effective when collective responses come from a broader context (Bayley, 1996). Eck and Maguire (2000) suggested that police should be considered a part of a network of institutions which can cumulatively influence crime. Perhaps, large agencies which specifically concentrate on identified problems and collaborate with other formal and informal institutions have a negative impact on crime as identified in this book. Why is this effect not observed in small agencies? In small communities, regardless of whether a written problem-solving agreement exists, community entities may be more likely to help law enforcement agencies solve safety related problems. By contrast, in large communities, only those agencies formally involved might collaborate with law enforcement agencies. This, in turn, might yield a significant difference among large communities. Given the significance level of this dimension, the results do not provide full support for the idea that the problem-solving partnership dimension is likely to have a crime reduction effect. Also, a crime reduction effect is not evident in the full and the small agency models.

POLICY IMPLICATIONS

This book did not find any evidence to justify the crime reduction effect of community policing. In contrast to the crime reduction expectation, the training and problem-solving dimension of community policing is associated with higher crime rates. However, these findings have to be scrutinized and interpreted within a broader context.

Even though one of the objectives of community policing is preventing crime, community policing seems more effective in reducing the fear of crime and in improving public relations (Cordner, 1997; Lindsey & McGilis, 1986; Police Foundation, 1981; Schneider, 1978; Trojanowicz, 1983). For these successes, community policing should be continued. Furthermore, it is observed that structural level factors are stronger predictors of crime rates in a community than community policing. In support to this argument, Sherman and Eck (2006) argued that the more powerful social institutions such as labor markets and the family make a more important contribution to crime prevention than any policing strategy. If collective awareness and response coming from a variety of social institutions target the crime problem in a community, then crime reduction is a reasonable expectation (Eck & Maguire, 2000). Therefore, it can be argued that community policing efforts are less likely to provide expected results (especially crime reduction) unless structural level indicators are improved in the community.

Through a careful review of previous evaluation studies, Sherman and Eck (2006) concluded that "community policing without a clear focus on crime risk factors generally shows no effect on crime" (p. 295). In this study, agencies implementing community policing to a greater extent might fail to address crime risk factors. If so, for the future, agencies utilizing community policing activities should consider crime risk factors when developing crime prevention strategies under the banner of community policing.

The literature consistently notes that many agencies adopted community policing without careful consideration of its philosophy, organizational change, and adequate training. As a result, many evaluation studies fail to reveal findings in support of community policing. This argument has merit for several reasons. First, the community policing initiative was fueled with federal grants without careful planning and consideration of its necessity. It is likely that if community policing is implemented in the way it is envisioned by scholars, it might achieve its objectives. The success of city specific programs such as CAPS, problem-solving in New York City, and community policing in Madison, Wisconsin might be related to the fact that these programs have been implemented in collaboration with policing scholars. Therefore, these programs were initiated in the way that they were planned. It is not suggested that every department find policing scholars and work with them, but implementing innovative strategies in the way that they are prescribed might increase the chances of success.

For large agencies, this study found that a problem-solving partnership is associated with lower violent crime rates. In more complex social environments, the importance of collaboration appears to yield a crime reduction effect. In that sense, large agencies should continue to expand their partnership with different community entities.

Although it was found that the training and problem-solving dimension is positively associated with crime rates, a community's needs should be taken into consideration in policing. In a democratic world, *"raison d'État"* must be determined according to the best interests of the public, not according to the interests of a few elites.

State services should target and be designed according to the best interests of community. Policing must be for the community and with the community. No actions of law enforcement agencies can be legitimate unless they are in harmony with the community's needs and interest.

LIMITATIONS AND DIRECTIONS FOR FUTURE STUDY

In all the published community policing research, the most common and important drawbacks are the lack of a solid theoretical background and agreed upon measures of community policing. Based on the items in the community policing section of the LEMAS survey, factor analyses provided a three-factor solution. Efforts to sustain the content and face validity of these three factors with two common definitions clouded rather than clarified the picture. Nevertheless, this book measured community policing more thoroughly than the previous research which utilized the LEMAS data.

Despite the research and expertise, it may be a little naïve to expect a unique community policing theory to emerge. This problem seems to continue to limit community policing studies. For example, Scott, Duffee, and Renauer (2003) contended that in the core of community policing, law enforcement agencies should strengthen a community's social control to take care of its own problems. However, as in many evaluation studies, this study lacks the measures that can assess this process. This book measured community policing through three dimensions. However, one of the core aspects of community policing which might have an effect on crime rates is not captured.

Second, only community policing related activities are included in the analyses, in part, because of the available data. Future studies might control for or examine the impact of other policing strategies which might be more strongly related to crime rates such as hot spots and directed patrols. In the same way, instead of using official crime rates which are subject to criticism, victimization data by itself or in conjunction with official crime data might illustrate a better picture of the relationship between community policing and crime.

Third, subjectivity and respondents' manipulation inherently limit the survey research's reliability and validity. The researcher attempted to identify the extent of the implementation of community policing with dichotomous items available in the LEMAS data. Even though the presence of community policing implementation is quantified to some extent through three composite measures, it is still uncertain to what extent each of the community policing activities is implemented in an agency. It is likely that variation in community policing activities among the agencies is plausible for each type of activity. For example, training citizens in community policing activities might range from simply distributing an informative brochure to an intensive training for a specified length of time. Future studies should attempt to capture the variation for the same type of activities among agencies. Moreover, this research, parallel with the literature, suggests that testing the effectiveness of community policing is more problematic at the aggregate level where there are many versions of the definition and implementation of community policing. A better strategy might be to examine these activities under the umbrella of community policing at the city level where the definition and implementation can be better identified.

Fourth, time-ordered cross-sectional design was used to examine the relationship between community policing and crime rates in this book. Cross-sectional design enabled the researcher to also explore the effect of community policing on crime rates for small agencies. However, since agencies often do not maintain a strategy long enough to show its effects, examining how long an agency's community policing activity lasts might be a better strategy. With the current data collection procedure of LEMAS, this is not viable. For each wave of data collection (every three years), LEMAS collects data from all agencies which have 100 or more sworn officers. The rest of the sample (agencies having fewer than 100 sworn officers) is drawn from a universe of small agencies for each data wave. In short, small agencies are not the same agencies in each wave. Therefore, a proper longitudinal design that encompasses all agencies that participate in the survey cannot be employed.

Finally, because of data restrictions, law enforcement agencies are used as the unit of analysis. Future studies, if possible, should utilize neighborhood level data to provide a better picture of possible variations within jurisdictions. Besides, demographical variables were gathered at one point in a time (Census 2000). Therefore, possible changes over time and their impacts cannot be precisely captured.

CONCLUDING REMARKS

Recently, Philadelphia Police Commissioner Ramsey unveiled a crime-fighting plan which includes increased community policing activity, putting more officers on foot and bike patrol along with a "stop and frisk" strategy, in an effort to reduce murders by 25%. When asked about this plan, Dr. Alex Piquero suggested that "the success of this plan depends on what the officer is doing on the street" (On foot, bike, and segway, 2008, p.33). Piquero's response demonstrates that how a policing strategy is viewed by scholars drastically differs from both how it is perceived at the political level and what happens on the street. In this regard, the difference between the rhetoric and reality of community policing are obvious. It is likely that politicians and police chiefs place more emphasis on the symbolic politics of community policing rather than its actual prescribed effects on neighborhoods. Although not much changes in the neighborhood in terms of crime and disorder, the friendly face of police departments garnished with a public relations campaign might promote a sense of safety especially for some community groups.

More radical approaches view community policing as a passive reform against disadvantaged groups in the society. Reed (1999) suggested that "… community policing sounds revolutionary if one accepts its rhetoric. However, it is reformist in nature and seeks to maintain the status quo in a capitalist society" (p. 133). In the same way, Herbert (2006) contended that as a result of a series of policies, disadvantaged groups got labeled as dangerous groups and deposited in prisons. In support of this political shift, the underlying objective of community policing (strengthen the ability of disadvantaged groups to take care of their own problems) reflected a neo-liberalist approach that withdrew state services from the least advantaged neighborhoods (p. 181). If these arguments about the politics of community policing have merit, inconclusive results about it effectiveness are not surprising.

Crime as a social phenomenon is influenced by many factors, all of which can not be included in a single study based on the current capabilities of social research. In short, social science continues to be limited in drawing conclusions about social phenomena. This book is neither the first nor the last word on the effectiveness of community policing. The conclusion drawn from this research is that the training and problem-solving dimension of community policing is associated with higher crime rates. Although plausible explanations about why this is the case are presented, it remains a puzzling research question for future research endeavors. Consequently, this book demonstrates that an innovative police response cannot be a unique contributor to a reduction in crime rates. However, if carefully and seriously implemented, it has the potential to be, at best, one of the contributing factors.

Notes

CHAPTER ONE

[1] In their studies, MacDonald used cities with population greater than 100,000; and Beckman used agencies having 100 or more full-time sworn officers.

[2] LEMAS 2003 is the latest version of the series available. It has been conducted in three year intervals since 1987.

CHAPTER THREE

[3] There were three types of evaluation design in this study: police community newsletters, victim re-contacts, and area-wide evaluation designs. Only the area-wide evaluations design is described in this study.

[4] Burglary dropped significantly, but no effect was found for robbery and theft.

[5] Storefronts and door to door visits did not produce a reduction in crime, yet visits coupled with a "Buy and Bust" program were found to be associated with a crime reduction.

CHAPTER FOUR

[6] 1 = four-year college, 2 = two-year college, 3 = some college but no degree, 4 = high school diploma or equivalent, 5 = no formal education. 4 and 5 are recoded as 0 referring to "no college degree"; 1, 2 and 3 are recoded as 1 referring to "some college degree".

CHAPTER FIVE

[7] The BTS highly depends on the sample size. Therefore, with large sample sizes, the result is very likely to be significant despite low correlations among variables (Tabachnick & Fidell, 2001).

[8] The process of cross matching is subject to the researcher's decision.

[9] Both significant and insignificant independent variables were depicted for each regression model for three reasons. First, elimination of insignificant predictors did not yield a drastic change. Second, since the significance of the predictor variables varies according to each regression model, the researcher would like the readers to follow the change in the significance of independent variables over the models. Third, according to the literature, insignificant variables such as education requirements for new recruits and the percentage of community policing officers are crucial factors that should be included in order to create comprehensive models. In addition, regression models were also undertaken by eliminating insignificant variables from the models. Both backward and stepwise regression analyses did not change any variable's significance. For a few control variables, minor changes were detected in their significance level. For example, if the variable is significant at the .05 level in the model that includes all independent variables, it turns out to be significant at the .01 level when insignificant variables are exluded. Therefore, the researcher chose to retain all independent variables in regression models.

References

Adams, R. E., Rohe, W. M., & Arcury, T. A. (2002). Implementing community-oriented policing: Organizational change and street officer attitudes. *Crime and Delinquency, 48*(3), 399-430.

Adams, R. E., Rohe, W. M., & Arcury, T. A. (2005). Awareness of community-oriented policing and neighborhood perceptions in five small to midsize cities. *Journal of Criminal Justice, 33*, 43-54.

Adamson, P. B. (1991). Some comments on the origin of the police. *Police Studies, 14*, 1-2.

Angell, J. (1971). Toward an alternative to the classic police organizational arrangement: A democratic model. *Criminology, 8*, 185-206

Bachman, R., & Schutt, R. K. (2001). *The practice of research in criminology and criminal justice.* Thousand Oaks, CA: Pine Forge Press.

Bayley, D. H. (1994). International differences in community policing. In D. P. Rosenbaum (Ed.), *The challenge of community policing* (pp. 278-281). Thousands Oak, CA: Sage.

Bayley, D. H. (1996). *The police for the future.* New York, Oxford University Press.

Bayley, D. H. (1998a). *What works in policing?* New York, Oxford University Press.

Bayley, D. H. (1998b). *Policing in America: Assessment and prospects.* Washington DC: Police Foundation.

Beckman, K. A. (2006). Community policing and changing crime rates: Does what police do matter? *Masters Abstracts International, 44*(05), 133. (UMI No.1433715).

Benedict, W. R., Bower, D. J., Brown, B., & Cuningham, R. (1999). Small town surveys: Bridging the gap between police and the community. *Journal of Contemporary Criminal Justice, 15* (2), 144-154.

Bennett, R. R., & Wiegand, R.B. (1994). Observations on crime reporting in a developingnation. *Criminology, 32* (1), 135-148.

Blumstein, A., & Wallman, J. (2000). *The crime drop in America.* New York, Cambridge University Press.

Bowers, W. J. & Hirsch, J.H. (1987). The impact of foot patrol staffing on crime and disorder in Boston: An unmet promise. *American Journal of Police,* 6, 17-44.

Bowling, B., & Foster, J. (2002). Policing and the police. In M. Maguire, R. Morgan, & R. Reiner (Eds.), *The Oxford handbook of criminology* (pp.421-460), Oxford: Clarendon Press.

Braga, A. A., & Weisburd, D. L. (2006). *Police innovation and crime preventionLessons learned from police research over the past 20 years.* Washington, DC: National Institute of Justice.

Brand, M. W. & Birzer, M. L. (2003). The benefits of community policing in rural Oklahoma. In Q. C. Thurman & E. F. McGarrel (Eds.), *Community policing in a rural setting* (pp. 105-112). Cincinnati, OH: Anderson Publishing.

Brown, L. P. (1989). *Community policing*: A practical guide for police officials. Washington, DC: National Institute of Justice.

Bureau of Justice Statistics (2006). *Law enforcement management and administrative statistics 2003: Sample survey of law enforcement agencies.* Washington, DC: Author.

Burgess, R. L., & Akers, R. L. (1966). A differential association-reinforcement theory of criminal behavior. *Social Problems, 14,* 128-147.

Bursik, R. J.,& Grasmick, H. G. (1993). *Neighborhoods and crime: The dimensions of Effective community control.* Lanham, MD: Lexington.

Butterfield, R., Edwards, C., & Woodall, J. (2005). The new public management and managerial roles: The case of the police sergeant. *British Journal of Management.*16, 329–341.

Carter, D. L., & Radelet, L. A. (1999). *The police and the community* (6th ed). Upple Saddle River, NJ: Prentice Hall.

Carter, D. L., & Sapp A. D. (1998). Community policing evaluation. In L. T. Hoover (Ed.), *Police program evaluation* (pp. 57-127). Washington, DC: Police   Executive Research Forum.

Champion, D. J. (2000). *Research methods for criminal justice and criminology* (2nd ed). Upple Saddle River, NJ: Prentice Hall.

Champion, D. J., & Rush, G. E. (1997). *Policing in the community*. Upple Saddle River, NJ: Prentice Hall.

Chappell, A. T., Lanza-Kaduce, L., & Johnston, D. H. (2005). Law enforcement training: Changes and challenges. In R. G. Dunham and G. P. Alpert (Eds.), *Critical issues   in policing* (pp. 71-88). Long Grove, IL: Waveland Press.

Campbell, R.T. (1992). Longitudinal research. In E. Borgatta & M. Borgatta (Eds), *Encyclopedia of Sociology*. New York. Macmillan.

Chapman, R. (2008). Community policing nugget: How planning and research units can do more to promote innovation and advance community policing. *Community Policing Dispatch, 1 (6)*. Retrieved June 3, 2008 from http://www.cops.usdoj.gov/html/dispatch

Cheurprakobkit, S. (2002). Community policing: Training, definitions and policy implications. *Policing: An International Journal of Police Strategies and   Management, 25*(4), 709–725.

Clinard, M. B. (1964). *Anomie and deviant behavior*, NewYork: Free Press

Cloward, R. A., & Ohlin, L. E. (1960). *Delinquency and opportunity*. Glencoe, Ill: Free Press of Glencoe.

Cole, David. (1999). *No equal justice*. New York: The New Press.

Colvin, C. A., & Goh, A. (2006). Elements underlying community policing: Validation of the construct. *Police Practice and Research*. 7 (1), 19–33.

Community Policing Consortium. (1994). *Understanding community policing: A framework for action*. Washington, DC: Bureau of Justice Assistance.

Cordner, G. W. (1988). A problem-oriented approach to community-oriented policing. In J. Greene & S. Mastrofski (Eds.), *Community Policing: Rhetoric or Reality* (pp. 135-152). New York: Praeger.

Cordner, G. W. (1997). Community policing: Elements and effects. In G. P Alpert and A. Piquero (Eds.), *Community policing: Contemporary readings* (pp. 451-468). Prospect Heights, IL: Waveland Press.

Cordner, G. W. & Biebel, E. P. (2005). Problem-oriented policing in practice. *Criminology & Public Policy, 4*, 155-180.

Cordner, G. W. & Scarborough, K. E. (2003). Operationalizing community policing in rural America: Sense and nonsense. In Q. C. Thurman & E. F. McGarrel (Eds.), *Community policing in a rural setting* (pp. 11-20). Cincinnati, OH: Anderson Publishing.

Cudeck, R. (2000). Exploratory factor analysis. In H. E, A, Tinsley S,   D. Brown (Eds.), *Handbook of applied multivariate statistics and mathematical modeling (pp.* 265-296). San Diego, CA: Academic Pres

Cullen, F. T., & Agnew, R. (2004). *Criminological theory: Past to present* (2nd ed.). Los Angeles: Roxbury Publishing.

Davis, R. C. & Maxwell, C. (2003). *Preventing repeat incidents of family violence: A reanalysis of data from three field tests.* Washington, DC: National Institute of Justice.

Denhardt R. B. & Denhardt, J. V. (2000). The new public service: Serving rather than steering. *Public Administration Review. 60 (6),* 549-561.

Department of Justice. (1973). *Improving Police/Community Relations.* Washington, DC: U.S. Government Printing Office.

DeVellis, R. F. (2003). *Scale development: theory and applications.* Thousands Oak, CA: Sage.

Duman, A. (2007). *Contingency paradox for police organizations.* Saarbrucken, Germany: VDM Verlag Publishing.

Eck, J. E. (1992). Criminal investigation. In G. W. Cordner & D.C. Hale (Eds), *What works in policing? Operations and administration examined* (pp. 31-52). Cincinnati, OH: Anderson Publishing.

Eck J. E., & Spelman, W. (1987a). Who ya gonna call: The police as problem busters. *Crime and Delinquency, 33,* 31-52.

Eck J. E., & Spelman, W. (1987b). *Problem solving: Problem-oriented policing in Newport News.* Washington, DC: Police Executive Research Forum.

Eck, J. E., & Maguire, E. R. (2000). Have changes in policing reduced violent crime? An assessment of the evidence. In A. Blumstein & J. Wallman (Eds), *The crime drop in America* (pp 207-265). New York: Cambridge University Press.

Ellis, L., & Walsh, A. (2007). *Criminology: A global perspective.* Needham Heights, MA: Allyn and Bacon.

Federal Bureau of Investigation. (2004). *Uniform crime reporting handbook.* Clarksburg,WV: Author.

Federal Bureau of Investigation. (2007, September). *Crime in the United States.*Retrieved   October,   5,   2007 http://www2.fbi.gov/ucr/cius2006/offenses/

Fielding, N. G. (2005). Concepts and theory in community policing. *The Howard* Journal, *44* (5), 460-472.

Fowler, F. J., McCalla, M. E., & Mangione, T. W. (1979). *Reducing residential crime and fear: The Hardford neighborhood crime prevention program.* Washington, DC: Department of Justice.

Freund, R. J., & Wilson, W. J. (1998). *Regression analysis: Statistical modeling of a response variable.* Chestnut Hill, MA: Academic Press.

Fridell, L., & Wycoff, M. A. (2004). *The results of three national surveys on community policing.* Washington, DC: Police Executive Research Forum.

Friedmann, R.R. (1990). Community policing: Promises and challenges. *Journal of Contemporary Criminal Justice.* 6 (2), 79-88.

Garson, D. G. (2008). *Factor Analysis.* Retrieved April 9, from http://www2.chass.ncsu.edu/garson/pa765/factor.htm#category

General Accounting Office. (1995). *Community policing: Information on the "cops on the beat" grant program.* Washington, DC: Author.

Germann, A. C. (1969). Community policing: An assessment. *Journal of Criminal Law, Criminology, and Police Science, 60,* 89-96.

Gest, T. (2001). *Crime & politics : Big government's erratic campaign for law and order.* New York: Oxford University Press.

Giacomazzi, A. L. & McGarrell, E. F. (2002). Using multiple methods in community crime prevention and community-policing research: the case of project ROAR. In M. Morash and J. K. Ford (Eds.), *The move to community policing: Making change happen* (pp.61-78). Thousands Oak CA: Sage Publications.

Glensor, R., Carreio, M., & Peak, K. (2000). *Policing communities.* Los Angeles, Roxbury Publishing.

Goldstein, H. (1977). *Policing a free society.* New York: HarpinCollins Publishing.

Goldstein, H. (1987). Toward Community-Oriented Policing. *Crime & Delinquency, 33*(1), 6-30.

Goldstein, H. (1990). *Problem-oriented policing.* New York: McGraw-Hill.

Government Accountability Office. (2003). *Technical assessment of Zhao and Thurman's 2001 evaluation of the effects of cops grants on crime, June, 2003.* Washington, DC: Author.

Government Accountability Office. (2005). *Interim report on the effects of cops funds on the decline in crime during the 1990s, June, 2005.* Washington, DC: Author.

Green, L. (1995). Cleaning up drug hot spots in Oakland, California: The displacement and diffusions effect. *Justice Quarterly, 12,* 737-754.

Green-Mazerolle, L. & Terril, W. (1997). Problem-oriented policing in public housing: Identifying the distribution of problem places. *Policing, 20,* 235-255.

Greene, J. R. (1999). Zero Tolerance: A case study of police policies and practices in New York City. *Crime and Delinquency, 45*(2), 171-187.

Greene, J. R. (2000). Community policing in America: changing the nature, structure, and the function of the police. In J. Horney (Ed.), *Policies, processes, and the decisions of the criminal justice system* (pp. 299-370). Washington, DC: National Institute of Justice.

Greene, J. R. & Mastrofski, S. D. (1988). *Community policing: Rhetoric or reality.* New York: Prager Publishers.

Greene, J. R. & Taylor, R. B. (1988). Community based policing and foot patrol: Issue of theory and evaluation. In J. R. Greene & S. D. Mastrofski (Eds.), *Community Policing: Rhetoric or Reality* (pp. 195-223). New York: Praeger.

Haberfeld, M. R. (2002). *Critical issues in training.* Upper Saddle River, NJ: Prentice-Hall.

Hart, T. C., & Rennison, C. (2003). *Reporting crime to the police, 1992-2000.* Washington, DC: Bureau of Justice Statistics.

Hawkins, C. W. & Weisheit, R. A. (2003). The state of community policing in small towns and rural areas. In Q. C. Thurman & E. F. McGarrel (Eds.), *Community policing in a rural setting* (pp. 21-29). Cincinnati, OH: Anderson Publishing.

Heimer, K., & Coster, S. (1999). The gendering of violent delinquency. *Criminology, 37* (2), 277- 318.

Herbert, S. (2006) Policing the contemporary city: Fixing broken windows or shoring up neo-liberalism. In V. E. Kappeler (Ed.), *The Police and The Society.* (pp. 168-188) Long Grove, IL: Waveland Press 168-188

Hickman, M. J., & Reaves, B. A. (2003). *Local police departments 2000.* Washington, DC: Department of Justice.

Hickman, M. J., & Reaves, B. A. (2006). *Local police departments 2003.* Washington, DC: Department of Justice.

Hickman, M. J., Piquero, A. R., Greene, J. R. (2000). Does community policing generate greater numbers and different types of citizen complaints than traditional policing? *Police Quarterly. 3*(1), 70-84.

Hirschi, T., & Gottfredson, M. (1983). Age and the explanation of crime. *American Journal of Sociology, 89*, 552-584.

Hoggett, P. (1996). New modes of control in the public service. *Public Administration.*74, 9–32.

Hood, C. (1995). The "new public management" in the eighties. *Accounting, Organization and Society.* 20 (2), 93- 109.

Hoyle, R. H., & Duvall, J. L. (2004). Determining the number of factors in exploratory and confirmatory factor analysis. In D. Kaplan (Ed.),

Handbook of quantitative methodology for the social sciences (pp. 301-315). Thousand Oaks, CA: Sage Publications.

Hunter, R. D., & Barker, T. (1993). BS and buzzwords: The new police organizational style. *American Journal of Police, 12,* 157-168.

Johnson, D. R. (1981). *American Law Enforcement History.* St. Louis, MO: Forum press.

Kappeler, V. E. & Gaines, L. K. (2005). *Community policing: A contemporary perspective.* Cincinnati, OH: Anderson Publishing.

Katz v. United States, 389 U.S. 347 (1967).

Keith, G. (2000). University policing and the community. *Law and Order.* 48 (12), 111-117.

Kelling, G. L., & Moore, M. H. (1988). *The Evolving Strategy of Policing, Perspectives on Policing:* U.S. Department of Justice, National Institute of Justice.

Kennedy, L. W., & Veitch, D. (1997). Why are crime rates going down? A case study in Edmonton, *Canadian Journal of Criminology, 39* (1), 51-69.

Kessler, D. A., & Duncan, S. (1996). The impact of community policing in four Houston neighborhoods. *Evaluation Review, 20*(6), 627-669.

Kim, J. O., & Mueller, C. W. (1978). *Factor Analysis: Statistical methods and practical issues.* Thousand Oaks, CA: Sage Publications.

King, W. R., & Lab, S. P. (2000). Crime prevention, community policing, and training: Old wine in new bottles. *Police Practice and Research, 1* (2), 242-252.

Kornhauser, R. (1978). *Social sources of delinquency.* Chicago: University of Chicago Press.

Kraska, P. B. & Neuman, W. L. (2007) *Criminal justice and criminology research methods.* Boston: Allyn & Bacon.

Lab, S. P. & Das, D. K. (2003). *International perspectives on community policing and crime prevention.* Upple Saddle River, NJ: Prentice Hall.

LaFree, G. (1998). Social institutions and crime bust of the 1990s. *The Journal of Criminal Law in Criminology,* 88, 1325-1368.

Lance, C. E., Butts, M. M., & Michels, L. C. (2006). The sources of four commonly reported cutoff criteria: What did they really say? *Organizational Research Methods, 9* (2), 202-220.

Lautenschlager, G. J. (1988). Determining the number of principal components to retain via parallel analysis: Alternatives to Monte Carlo analyses, *Paper presented at the Annual Meeting of the American Psychological Association Atlanta, GA, August 12-16, 1988* (96th).

Law Enforcement Agency Identifiers Crosswalk. (2000). Retrieved July 28, 2007,from ttp://www.icpsr.umich.edu/cocoon/ICPSR/STUDY/04082.xml

Law Enforcement Management and Administrative Statistics (2003). Retrieved July 28, 2007, from http://www.icpsr.umich.edu/cocoon/ICPSR/STUDY /04411.xml

Leech, N. L., Barret, K. C., & Morgan, G. A. (2005). *SPSS for intermediate statistics:Use and interpretation*. Mahwah, NJ: Lawrence Earlbaum Publishers.

Leighton, B. N. (1991). Visions of community policing: Rhetoric and reality in Canada. *Canadian Journal of Criminology, July-October*, 485-522.

Levitt, S. (1997). Using electoral cycles in police hiring to estimate the effect ofpolice on crime. *American Economic Review, 87*, 270-290.

Lilley, D. & Hinduja, S. (2006). Organizational values and police officer evaluation: A content comparison between traditional and community policing agencies. *Police Quarterly, 9* (4), 486–513.

Lilley, D. R. (2006). Assessing jurisdiction-level crime trends during the 1990s: An analysis of the impact of policing changes. *Dissertation Abstracts International, 67* (05), 259. (UMI No. 3216148)

Lindgren, S. A. & Zawitz, M. W. (2001). *Linking Uniform Crime Reporting Data to Other Datasets*. Washington, DC: Bureau of Justice Statistics.

Loftin, C., & McDowall, D. (1998). The police, crime and economic theory: An asesment. In D. H. Bayley (Ed.), *What works in policing* (pp. 10-25). New York: Oxford Unversity Press.

Lurigio, A. J., & Rosenbaum, D. P. (1986). The evaluation research in community crime prevention. A critical look in the field. In D. P. Rosenbaum (Ed.), *Community crime prevention: Does it work* (pp. 19-44). Beverly Hills, CA: Sage Publications.

Lyn, H. (2007). Building police youth relationships: The importance of procedural justice. *Youth Justice, 7* (3), 195-209.

MacDonald, J. M. (2002). The effectiveness of community policing in reducing urban violence. *Crime & Delinquency, 48*(4), 592-618.

Maguire, E. R., & Katz, C. M. (2002). Community policing, loose coupling and sensemaking in American police agencies. *Justice Quarterly*, 19(3): 503-536.

Maguire, E. R., Mastrofski, S. P. (2000). Patterns of community policing. *Police Quarterly*. 3(1), 4-45.

Maguire, E. R., Kuhns, J. B., Uchida, C. D., & Cox, S. M. (1997). Patterns of community policing in nonurban America. *Journal of Research in Crime and Delinquency, 34*, 368-394.

Maguire, E. R., & Uchida, C. D. (1998). Measuring community policing at the precinct and agency levels. *Paper presented at the annual meeting of the American Society of Criminology, Washington, DC, Nov 14, 1998.*

Maguire, E. R., Kuhns, J. B., Uchida, C. D., & Cox, S. M. (2000). Measuring community policing at the agency level. *Unpublished manuscript, George Mason University.*

Manning, P. (1984). Community policing. *American Journal of Police, 3*(2), 205–227.

Mapp v. Ohio, 367 U.S. 643 (1961).

Marion, N. (1998). Police academy training: Are we teaching recruits what they need to know? *Policing, 21* (1), 54-75.

Markowitz, F. E., & Felson, B. R. (1998). Social-demographic attitudes and violence. *Criminology 36* (1), 117–138.

Marvell, T. & Moody, C. (1996). Specification problems, police levels, and crime rates. *Criminology, 34* (2), 609-646.

Mastrofski, S. D. (1999). *Ideas in American Policing: Policing for people.* Washington, DC: Police Foundation.

Mastrofski, S. (2006). Community policing: A skeptical view." In D. L. Weisburd and A. A. Braga (Eds.), *Police innovation: Contrasting perspectives* (pp. 44-76). New York: Cambridge University Press.

Mastrofski, S. D., Parks, R. B., Reiss, A. J., & Worden, R. E. (1999). *Policing neighborhoods: A report from St. Petersburg.* Washington, DC: National Institute of Justice.

Mastrofski, S. D., Parks, R., & Worden, R. (1998). *Community policing in action:*

Lessons from an observational study. Washington, DC: National Institute of Justice.

Matthews, R. (1992). Replacing broken windows: Crime, incivilities, and urban change. In R. Matthews & J. Young (Eds.), *Issues in realist criminology* (pp. 19-50). London, Sage Publications.

Mazerolle, L. G., Ready, J., Terrill, W., Waring, E. (2000). Problem oriented policing in public housing: The Jersey City evaluation. *Justice Quarterly, 17* (1), 129-159.

McGarrel, E. F., Benitez, S. & Gutierrez, R. S. (2003). Getting to know your community through citizen surveys and focus group interviews. In Q. C. Thurman & E. F. McGarrel (Eds.), *Community policing in a rural setting* (pp. 113-121). Cincinnati, OH: Anderson Publishing.

Mernard, S. (2002). *Longitudinal research.* Thousand Oaks, CA: Sage Publications.

Mertler, C. A., & Vannatta, R. A. (2005). *Advanced and multivariate statistical methods:practical application and interpretation.* Glendale, CA: Pyrczak Publishing.

Messner, S. (1982). Poverty, inequality, and the urban homicide rate. *Criminology, 20,* 103-114.

Miethe, T. D. (2007). *Simple statistics: Applications in criminology and criminal justice.* Los Angeles: Roxbury Publishing.

Miller, L. S. & Hess, K. M. (2002). *The police in the community: Strategies for the 21st century* (3rd ed). Belmont, CA: Wadsworth.

Miranda v. Arizona, 384 U.S. 436 (1966).

Montgomery, D. C., Peck, E. A., & Vining, G. G. (2005). *Introduction to linear regression analysis.* New York: Wiley Interscience.

Moore, M. H. (1994). Research synthesis and policy implications. In D. P. Rosenbaum (Ed.), *The challenge of community policing* (pp. 285-299). Thousand Oaks, CA: Sage.

Muhlhausen, 2001, D. (2001). *Do community oriented policing services grants affect violent crime rates?* Washington, DC: Heritage Foundation.

National Advisory Commission on Civil Disorders. (1968). *Report.* Washington, DC: Government Printing Office.

National Commission on Law Observance and Enforcement (1931). *Report on lawlessness in law enforcement.* (Report No. 11). Washington, DC: U.S. Government Printing Office.

Novak, K. J., Alarid, L. F., & Lucas, W. L. (2003). Exploring officers' acceptance of community policing: Implications for policy implications. *Journal of Criminal Justice, 31 (1),* 57-71.

Norusis, M.J. (2000). *Guide to data analysis.* Upper Saddle River, NJ: Prentice Hall.

Nunnally. J. C., & Berstein, I. H. (1994). *Psychometric theory.* New York: McGraw-Hill.

Office of Community Oriented Policing Services. (2000). *Shared understanding of community policing.* Retrieved September, 12, 2007 from http://www.cops.usdoj.gov

Oliver, W. M. (2000). The third generation of community policing: Moving through innovation, diffusion, and institutionalization. *Police Quarterly.* 3(4), 367-388.

Omnibus Crime Control and Safe Streets Act, 42 U.S.C. § 3789d (1968).

On foot, bike and segway. (2008, February 9). *The Economist,* p. 33.

Ortmeier, P.J. (2002). *Policing the community: A guide for patrol operations.* Upper Saddle River, NJ: Prentice Hall.

Osgood, D. W. & Chambers, L. M. (2000). Social disorganization outside the metropolis: An analysis of rural youth violence. *Criminology, 23* (2), 81-114.

Pallant, J. (2005). *SPSS survival manual.* New York, McGraw-Hill.

Palmiotto, M. J. (2000). *Community policing: A policing strategy for the 21st century.* Gaithersburgh, MD: Aspen Publication.

Palmiotto, M. J., & Donahue, M. E. (1995). Evaluating community policing: Problems and prospects. *Police Studies, 18*(2), 33-53.

Pate, A. M., McPherson, M., Silloway, G. (1987). *The Minneapolis community crime prevention experiment.* Washington, DC: Police Foundation.

Pate, A. M. & Shtull, P. (1994). Community policing grows in Brooklyn: An inside view of New York City police department's model precinct. *Crime and Delinquency, 40 (*3), 381-410.

Pate, A. M. & Skogan, W. (1985). *Coordinated community policing: The Newark experience.* Washington, D.C: Police Foundation.

Pate, A. M., Wycoff. M. A., Skogan, W.G., & Sherman, L. W. (1986) *Reducing fear of crime in Houston and Newark: A summary report.* Washington, D.C: Police Foundation.

Peak, K. J. & Glensor, R. W. (2004).*Community policing and problem solving: Strategies and practices.* (4th ed). Upper Saddle River, NJ: Prentice Hall.

Pelfrey, W. V., Jr. (2004). The inchoate nature of community policing: Differences between community policing and traditional police officers. *Justice Quarterly, 21(3),* 579-601.

Police Foundation (1981). *The Newark Foot Patrol Experiment.* Washington, DC: Police Foundation.

President's Commissions on Law enforcement and Administration of Justice (1967). *The challenges of Crime in a Free Society.* Washington, DC: Government Printing Office.

Quinney, R. (1973). Crime control in capitalist society: A critical philosophy of legal order. *Issues in Criminology, 8,* 75-95.

Reaves, B. A. & Hickman, M. J. (2005). Census of state and local law enforcement agencies, 200, and LEMAS, 2000- highlights. In R. G. Dunham and G. P. Alpert (Eds.), *Critical issues in policing* (pp. 41-70). Long Grove, IL: Waveland Press.

Redlinger, L. J. (1994). Community policing and changes in the organizational structure. *Journal of Contemporary Criminal Justice, 10* (1), 36-59

Reinard, J. C. (2006). *Communication research statistics.* Thousands Oak, CA: Sage Publications.

Reisig, M. D. (2002). Citizen input and police service: Moving beyond the feel good community survey. In M. Morash and J. K. Ford (Eds.), *The move to community policing: Making change happen* (pp.61-78). Thousands Oak, CA: Sage Publications.

Reisig, M. D. & Parks, R. B. (2004). Can community policing help the truly disadvantaged? *Crime and Delinquency. 50* (2), 139-167.

Reitzel, J. D., Piquero, N. L., & Piquero, A. R. (2005). Problem-oriented policing. In R. G. Dunham and G. P. Alpert (Eds.), *Critical issues in policing* (pp. 419-431). Long Grove, IL: Waveland Press.

Ren, L., Cao, L., Lovrich, N., & Gaffney, M. (2005). Linking confidence in the police with the performance of the police: Community policing can make a difference. *Journal of Criminal Justice, 33*, 55-66.

Riechers, L. M., & Roberg, R. R. (1990). Community policing: A critical review of underlying assumptions. *Journal of Police Science and Administration, 17(2),* 105-114.

Robert, D. & Maxwell, C. (2003). *Preventing repeat incidents of family violence. A reanalysis of data from three field tests.* Washington, DC: National Institute of Justice.

Robert, D. & Taylor, B. G. (1997). A proactive response to family violence: The results of a randomized experiment. *Criminology, 35* (2), 307-333.

Robinson, C. D., Scaglion, R., & Olivero, J. M. (1994). *Police in contradiction: The evolution of the police function in society.* Westport, CT: Greenwood Press.

Rooh, S. & Oliver, W. M. (2005). Effects of community policing upon fear of crime: Understanding the causal linkage. *Policing: An International Journal of Police Strategies & Management, 28* (4), 670-683.

Rosenbaum, D. P. (1986). *Community crime prevention: Doest it work?* Beverly Hills: CA, Sage Publications.

Rosenbaum, D. P. (1987). The theory and research behind neighborhood watch: Is it a sound fear and crime reduction strategy? *Crime & Delinquency, 33*(1), 103-134.

Rosenbaum, D. P. (1988). The changing role of the police: Assessment of the current transition to community policing. In J. P. Bodeur (Ed.), *How to recognize good policing: Problems and issues* (pp. 27-53). Thousands Oak: CA, Sage Publications.

Rosenbaum, D. P. (1994). *The challenge of community policing: Testing the promises.* Thousand Oaks, CA: Sage Publications.

Roth, J. A. & Ryan, J. F. (2000). *The national evaluation of the cops program.* Washington, DC: National Institute of Justice.

Roth, J. A., Roehl, J., & Johnson, C. C. (2004). Trends in adaptation of community policing. In W. G. Skogan (Ed.), *Community policing: Can it work* (pp. 3-29). Belmont, CA: Wadsworth.

Sacco, V. F. (2005). *When crime waves.* Thousands Oak, CA: Sage Publications.

Sampson, R. (1987). Urban black violence: The effect of male jobelessness and family disruption. *American Journal of Sociology, 93,* 348-382.

Sampson, R. L, & Groves, W. B. (1989). Community structure and crime: Testing social disorganization theory. *The American Journal of Sociology, 94(4),* 774-802.

Sampson, R. L., & Raudenbush, S. W. (1999). Systematic social observation of public places: A new look at disorder in urban neighborhoods. *The American Journal of Sociology, 105* (3), 603-631.

Sampson, R. L, & Raudenbush, S. W., Earls, F. (1997) Neighborhoods and violence crime. A multilevel study of collective efficacy. *Science, 277,* 918-924.

Sampson, R. J., & Wilson. J. (1995).Toward a theory of race, crime, and urban inequality. In J. Hagan & R. Peterson (Eds.), *Crime and inequality* (pp. 37-54). Palo Alto, CA: Stanford University Press.

Schnebly, S. M. (2008).The influence of community-oriented policing on crime reporting behavior. *Justice Quarterly, 25* (2), 223-251.

Schneider, A. L. (1978). *The Portland forward records check of crime victims.* Washington, DC: Government Printing Office.

Scott, J. D., Duffee, D. E., & Renauer, B. C. (2003). Measuring police-community coproduction: the utility of community policing case studies. *Police Quarterly, 6* (4), 410-439.

Shaw, C. R., & McKay, H.D. (1942). Juvenile Delinquency and Urban Areas. In F. T. Cullen & R. Agnew (Eds.), *Criminological theory: Past to Present (Essential Readings)* (2nd ed., pp. 104-110). Los Angeles: Roxbury Publishing Company.

Sherman, D. & Eck, J. E. (2006). Policing for crime prevention. In L. W. Sherman, D. P. Farrington, B. C. Welsch & D. L. Mac Kenzie (Eds.), *Evidence-based crime prevention* (pp. 331-403). New York: Routledge.

Sherman, L. W., Farrington, D. P., Welsch, B. C., & Mac Kenzie, D. L. (2006). *Evidence-based crime prevention.* New York: Routledge.

Skogan, W. G. (2004). *Community policing: Can it work.* Belmont, CA: Wadsworth.

Skogan, W. G. (2006). *Police and the community in Chicago.* New York: Oxford University Press.

Skolnick, J. & Bayley, D. (1988). *Community policing: Issues and practices throughout the world.* Washington, DC: National Institute of Justice.

Smith, B. W., Novak, K. J., & Frank, J. (2001). Community policing and the work routines of street-level officers. *Criminal Justice Review, 26* (1), 17-38.

Stevens, D. J. (2003). *Applied community policing in the 21st century.* Boston: A and B Publishing.

Sozer, M. A. (2002). Total quality management: The standards of ISO 9000.*Police Journal,* 30, 85-87.

Tabachnick, B. G., & Fidell, L. S. (2001). *Using multivariate statistics.* New York: HarperCollins.

Tien, J. M. & Cahn, M. F. (1986). The commercial security field test program: A systematic evaluation of security surveys in Denver, St. Louis, and long Beach. In D. P. Rosenbaum (Ed.), *Community crime prevention: Does it work* (pp. 228-250). Beverly Hills, CA: Sage Publications.

Tilley, N. (2004). Community policing and problem solving. In W. G. Skogan (Ed.), *Community policing: Can it work* (pp. 165-184). Belmont, CA: Wadsworth.

Tinsley, H. E. A., & Tinsley, D. J. (1987). Uses of factor analysis in counseling psychology research. *Journal of Counseling Psychology, 34,* 414-424.

Trojanowicz, R. C. (1983). An evaluation of a neighborhood foot patrol program. *Journal of Police Science and Administration, 11*(4), 410-419.

Trojanowicz, R. C. (1994). *Community policing:* A survey of police departments in US. Washington, DC: Department of Justice.

Trojanowicz, R., & Bucqueroux, B. (1994). *Community policing: How to get started.* Cincinnati, OH: Anderson.

Turk, A. T. (1966). Conflict and criminality. *American Sociological Review, 31,* 338-352.

Uchida, C. D., Forst, B., & Annan, S. O. (1992). *Modern policing and the control of illegal drugs: Testing new strategies in two American cities.* Washington, DC: National Institute of Justice.

U.S. Census Bureau. (2001). *Introduction to Census 2000 Data Products.* Washington, DC: Author.

Uniform Crime Reporting Program Data. (2003). Retrieved July 28, 2007, from http://www.icpsr.umich.edu/cocoon/ICPSR/STUDY/04360.xml

Vinzant, J., & Crothers, L. (1994). Street-level leadership: the role of patrol officers in community policing. *Criminal Justice Review, 19* (2), 189-212.

Vito, G. F., Walsh, W. F., & Kunselman, J. (2005). Community policing: The middle manager's perspective. *Police Quarterly,* 8 (4), 490–511.

Violent Crime Control and Law Enforcement Act, 18 U.S.C. §§ 1033-1034 (1994).

Walker, S. & Katz, C. M. (2005). *The police in America: An introduction* (5ᵗʰ ed). New   York, Mc GrawHill.

Walsh, W. F. (2005). Compstat: An analysis of an emerging police managerial paradigm. In R. G. Dunham, G. P. Alpert (Eds.), *Critical issues in policing: Contemporary readings* (pp. 201-216). Long Grove: IL, Waveland Press.

Warner, R. M. (2008). *Applied statistics.* Thousands Oak, CA: Sage.

Weatheritt, M. (1988). Community policing: Rhetoric or reality. In J. Greene & S. Mastrofski (Eds.), *Community policing: Rhetoric or reality* (pp. 153-177). New York: Praeger.

Weisburd, D., & J. Eck. (2004). "What can police do to reduce crime, disorder, and fear?" *Annals of the American Academy of Political and Social Science, 593,* 42- 65.

Weisheit, R. A. (1993). Studying drugs in rural areas: Notes from the field. *Journal of Research in Crime and Delinquency, 30,* 213-232.

Weisheit, R. A., Wells, L. E., Falcone, D. N. (1994). Community policing in small town   and rural America. *Crime and Delinquency. 40* (4), 549-567.

Wells, L. E. & Weisheit, R. A. (2004). Patterns of rural and urban crime: A county-level comparison. *Criminal Justice Review, 29* (1), 1-22.

White, M. D. (2007). *Current issues and controversies in policing.* Boston, A and B   Publishing.

Wilson, J. Q. (1975). *Thinking about crime.* New York: Metropolitan Books.

Wilson, J. Q. & Kelling, G. L. (March 1982). The police and neighborhood safety: Broken windows. *Atlantic Monthly, 249* (3), 29-37.

Wycoff, M. A. (1988). The benefits of community policing: Evidence and conjecture. In J. Greene & S. Mastrofski (Eds.), *Community Policing: Rhetoric or Reality* (pp. 103-120). New York: Praeger.

Wycoff, M. A. & Skogan, W. G. (1993). *Community policing in Madison: Quality from the inside out. An evalutaion of implementation and impact.* Technical Report. Washington, DC: Police Foundation.

Yin, R. K. (1986). A synthesis of eleven evaluations. In D. P. Rosenbaum (Ed.), *Community crime prevention: Does it work* (pp. 294-308). Beverly Hills, CA: Sage Publications.

Xu, Y., Fiedler, M. L., & Flaming, K. H. (2005). Discovering the impact of community policing: The broken windows thesis, collective efficacy, and citizens' judgment. *Journal of Research in Crime and Delinquency, 42* *(2),* 147-186.

Zawitz, M. W., Klaus, P. A., Bachman, R., Bastian, L.D., DeBarry, M.M. Jr., Rand, M. R., Taylor, B.M. (1993). *Highlights from 20 years of surveying crime victims: The national crime victimization survey, 1973-1992.* Washington, DC: Bureau of Justice Statistics.

Zhao, J. (1996). *Why police organizations change: A study of community oriented policing.* Washington, DC: Police Executive Research Forum.

Zhao, J., He, N., & Lovrich, N. P. (2003). Community policing: Did it change basicfunctions of policing in the 1990s. A national follow- up study. *Justice Quarterly, 20* (4), 697-725.

Zhao, J. S., Scheider, M. C., & Thurman, Q. (2002). Funding community policing to reduce crime: Have cops grants made a difference. *Criminology, 2* (1), 7-32.

Zhao, J. & Thurman, Q. (2004). *Funding community policing to reduce crime: Have COPS grants made a difference?* Washington, DC: Office of Community Oriented Policing Services.

Zhao, J., Thurman, Q. C., & Lovrich, N. P. (1995). Community-oriented policing across The U.S.: Facilitators and impediments to implementation. *American Journal of Police, 14,* 11-28.

Index